LINGUISTICS
FOR
COLLEGE
FRESHMEN AND SOPHOMORES

Non Majors, Welcome!

LINGUISTICS
FOR
COLLEGE
FRESHMEN AND SOPHOMORES

Non Majors, Welcome!

Gregory Shafer, Ph.D.

Robbie Dean Press   Ann Arbor, MI

Cover Design by John Meszaros

Printed in U.S.A.

ISBN: 1-889743-53-4

For making purchases online,
visit the online store of
MarketingNewAuthors.com
www.MarketingNewAuthors.com

To my wife for all of her patient encouragement

TABLE OF CONTENTS

INTRODUCTION

Language is not only the principal medium that human beings use to communicate with each other but also the bond that links people together and binds them to their culture. To understand our humanity we must understand the language that makes us human.

—*Language*, 4th edition

Despite the incredible significance of language to our lives and identity, few of us spend much time thinking about it. We talk before ever seeing a teacher and learn to read and write with most of the other kids in our grade school. As adults, we routinely use colorful metaphors to describe our feelings and quickly acclimate ourselves to the speech patterns of our friends or business colleagues. When it comes time to ask for directions from a man in a strange town, we are adept at changing the way we speak so as to get accurate directions. Each day, without thinking, we alter our diction to achieve success in formal and informal situations, tailoring our word choice to request a raise from our boss or more attention from our lover. And during all of these linguistic gymnastics, we rarely stop to consider our achievements. It is simply part of the every day rhythms that flow through our world.

Put simply, language is, perhaps, the most complex and yet least studied of the activities we do as humans. Like fish that move effortlessly through the water, we use language without reflecting on its social or personal impact. Despite this seeming indifference, there is little question of its incredible importance to our culture, personal identity, and professional success. Each day, language is a political cudgel, used to limit the power of others or to infuse an issue with life. Passionate prose are penned to revive the life of a personal goal or to stymie the hopes of a speaker who fails to fit the standard of the person in power. Dr. Martin Luther King, Jr. employed a mellifluous array of metaphors and analogies to reveal the racism of his time, elevating the topic for people who, otherwise, might not have appreciated the gravity of the situation. In a much different way, our nation has historically sought to stifle the progress of foreigners by suggesting that their language—like their culture—was uncivilized, savage, or immoral. Language has been used throughout history to strip Native Americans of their heritage, to make the less educated feel stupid, or to disrupt the voice of the minority speaker. And at the same time, it has been used to lift us from our chairs, to evoke tears.

It is only when we confront such acrimony or zeal that we begin to realize how critical language is to who we are. It is only when we feel the barb of someone making fun of our accent or ridiculing our word choice that we begin to recognize the fact that our language is interwoven with our persona. And so, we make decisions about how we speak, based on who we want to be and with whom we identify. Most of us have come to see certain styles of language as being superior to others, but such judgments will not stop us from speaking like the people we love and the community that has loved us.

"Don't go doin' that no more, or I'll have to hurt ya," warned a friend of mine after I offered her some candy from my desk. Her nonstandard English was crafted to show her friendly contempt for the fattening food and to demonstrate her ability to relax with me and talk in her own way. Later, she went to an English class and assumed the role of an ambitious and resourceful college senior, ready to handle an academic position, ready to discuss the diversity of our language. "We need to appreciate the myriad dialects and registers that flow through our society," she informed her teacher. Clearly, our friend was responding to the dynamics of the speech acts in which she found herself.

This book is written for such dynamic situations. While it attempts to provide information on important aspects of linguistic studies—and to include the ideas of significant people in the linguistic field—it's foremost an accessible and fun introduction to language. Too often, linguistics becomes a dry, lifeless walk through a thicket of arcane words and concepts. The personal and social importance of language becomes lost in convoluted discussions of semantic relevance and syntactical diagrams. For those who never seek a career in linguistics, I offer the following work. It strives to discuss topics that are germane to the life of every linguist and non-linguist and does so in a way that is comprehensible. It delves into dialects and registers and challenges long-held beliefs that certain ways of speaking are inherently better than others. It looks at the politics and history of language but does not attempt to cover each movement from Old English to modern discourse. It looks at the way we learn language and the social significance of words but never seeks to be a comprehensive authority on such daunting issues.

In short, it aspires to introduce all students to the exciting world of language. For too long this has been a field that has been approached with the same dread that one confronts the dentist. This prevents too many of us from delving into the facts about linguistics and the truth about speech acquisition and dialect development. As an introductory survey, this book seeks to touch upon issues and offer a background for further study. It endeavors to reveal the relevance of language, so others may explore this profession with more zest and commitment.

CHAPTER I

DIALECTS, LANGUAGE, POLITICS, AND YOU

It is estimated that between 5000 and 8000 languages exist in the world today. In the United States alone, there are approximately 230 different languages spoken.

—Valentine (35)

We live in a world of linguistic diversity. Not only are there hundreds of different languages around the globe but dozens of contrasting styles of how that language is spoken. Variation within a language is called dialect and helps to reveal the color of a language and the people who use it. We all speak both a dialect and registers of English and are capable of learning others, but there are political ramifications when we say that "we be going to church a lot lately" rather than "we have been in church a lot these past weeks." For most of us, dialects and registers are choices, but in deciding how we want to use language we make political decisions about the community of people with whom we want to associate and the image others will have of us. Language is personal, but it is also regional, social, and political.

In the southern part of the United States, Texans speak a dialect of English that is easily distinguishable from the Midwest or New England area. In the same way, some African Americans have developed a dialect that is distinctly different from White people of any region. And, of course, one can discern a great deal about people's educational background by listening to them speak. The man who sits at the diner and bemoans the politicians "who ain't got a lick of sense" can be quickly contrasted from the woman who laments "the total incompetence of our elected officials."

Of course, the formality of the English we speak is also influenced by the social context, and this introduces us to the notion of registers. In the classroom, anyone's speech tends to become more formal, more stuffy, while the picnic or softball game elicits a more informal, freer form of expression. Thus, all of us adjust our speech to fit the domain in which we speak. While people in the Midwest speak differently than those in the rural South, they all change their discourse to fit a particular context, which is what makes register unique. Simply put, language is a reflection of our heritage, our culture, our values, our educational background, and our social situation. The corporate attorney speaks a different register to his plumber than he does to his fellow attorney, to his child, or to his wife. The woman on the West Coast is discernible from the man in New England by the dialect they each speak. Dialects are the form of English we speak, while registers fluctuate to reflect the specific setting we find ourselves in. Consider the way you speak in the weight room. Now, consider your style of speech while discussing wedding plans with your priest, rabbi, minister, or other religious leader.

Language, Intelligence, and Pride

Despite what many would have us believe, language difference does not reflect intelligence. The high school dropout who proclaims that "life in the South ain't so bad" is simply using a different form of English than the college professor or medical doctor who suggests that "relocating to the South might not be as challenging as one might think." All of us employ a dialect to fit our values, society, and aspirations, and dialect use is as personal and legitimate as a family heirloom. Some might not appreciate its sounds and structure, but it serves the discourse community that uses it. Linguist Lisa Delpit tells us of a study involving Pima Indian children and their success in learning Standard

English at their school. As Delpit explains, by third grade the children had learned the English of their teachers but chose to use the "language of their local environment" (18), despite the stigma that went along with it. The researcher suggests that "by ages eight or nine the children had become aware of their group membership and its importance to their well-being and this realization was reflected in their language" (18-19). Put simply, the children knew how to approximate the language of power—of the teachers who taught them—but chose to speak like their families and to solidify the family connections they had through language.

Years ago, Martin Joos wrote a classic work on language variation titled *The Five Clocks*. Joos's premise was that language is situational and social and that variation is normal. A dialect or register does not expose ignorance or acumen but variety. Critical to his argument was the precept that schools must stop condemning dialects and registers simply because they do not replicate the formal discourse of the grammarian. "It is our custom unhesitatingly and unthinkingly," wrote Joos in deriding the notion of a monolithic speech pattern, "to demand that the clocks of language all be set to Central Standard Time. And each normal American is taught thoroughly, if not to keep accurate time, at least to feel ashamed whenever he notices that a clock of his is out of step with the English Department's tower clock" (4).

Research suggests that language and dialect use is often a choice that we make in deciding what kind of person we want to be and with whom we want to socialize. Rather than being related to intelligence, it reflects the devotion we feel to a certain community and our conscious desire to reject the language of those who have oppressed or embarrassed us. Linguist Signithia Fordham has argued that African-American children "lease" Standard English while in school as a way to please their instructors. Later, when class is dismissed, these same students return to their African American Vernacular English (AAVE) to socialize with friends and family. For all of these students, language is a choice and not a sign of intelligence. Fordham adds that language is often used by African-American students as a form of rebellion—that Black students strike back at the educational system by exulting their racial dialect and ostracizing those who try to be "White." For Fordham, language is used as an instrument of revolt and rebellion, a way to "diss" the system. "By using the standard only episodically between nine and three," writes Fordham, "the students display their awareness that it is deemed crucial to academic success. Further, by leasing rather than taking ownership of this school-approved discourse style, they also demonstrate their commitment to Ebonics and the prominent discourse practices in the African-American community" (275).

What we have to realize in examining dialects, registers, and the students who use them is that they are interwoven in their self perception—that learning a new way of speech is never a simple, dry, academic exercise. "Acquiring an additional code comes from identifying with the people who speak it, from connecting the language form with all that is self affirming and esteem building, inviting, and fun" (39) writes Lisa Delpit. When we learn a dialect, we do so for very personal reasons. When we refuse to learn one, it is also for reasons that far transcend any academic practice.

"A standard dialect," writes Harvey Daniels in response to questions about dialects and intelligence, "is not inherently superior to any other dialect of the same language. It may however confer considerable social, political, and economic power on its users, because of prevailing attitudes about the dialect's worthiness" (67).

While working in Miami, Florida in the 1980s, I saw the incredible power of language to move people to do—and undo—certain linguistic traditions. For many of the Cubans who populated the schools where I taught, learning Standard English was a critical part of becoming a true American—of making their journey to America complete. One of the most viable professions a person could pursue during this time was English instruction, since evening language classes to learn American English were springing up like flowers in a Miami garden. Cubans saw English as emblematic of democracy, freedom, and free enterprise and wanted to imbibe it the way a thirsty man guzzles water. This was not something to be "leased" for a short time but a new life, a changing part of their heritage and persona.

Such an example differs starkly from the woman who was moving to Alabama for a new job. In her feelings of trepidation over leaving her beloved New England, she declared that she would never give up her regional dialect and speak like those "hicks" in the South. Clearly, language has visceral meaning for most of us, and, whether or not we realize it, we speak like the community of people with whom we identify. It is not about intelligence but is a conscious choice by those who speak it and who see it as integral to who they are.

Language, People, and Power

This notion is evident in our nation's historical tendency to associate language with identity. When eighteenth-century America first contemplated the idea of being separate from England, its leaders began to examine their language and its relationship to their independence and mother country. Most leaders wanted to distinguish themselves from the tongue of the English and establish a discourse that was uniquely American. Most believed that languages mirrored the values and refinement of the people who spoke them, which meant that Americans must stop speaking like their English oppressors and adopt a discourse that was consonant with their democratic, earthy values.

And so, John Adams, America's second president, was one of the first to suggest that Americans establish an academy of language and propagate the nation's unique and moral way of communicating. For Adams and others like him, language was a way to showcase autonomy from British rule, to declare cultural freedom from the repressive, monarchial language of the mother country, and spread the "purity, copiousness, and perfection of language" (31) that was evinced in the American lexicon. During the Revolutionary War, Adams wrote a proposal for the creation of an American language academy, arguing that language was a reflection of the people, their manners, and distinctive character. "It is not to be disputed that the form of government has an influence upon language, and language in its turn influences not only the form of government but the temper, the sentiments, and manners of the people" wrote Adams (31).

Noah Webster was yet another proponent of this movement, suggesting that Americans must be liberated from England's language as well as her government. For both Adams and Webster, language was about much more than communication. It was a part of the nation's character and a vehicle to complete independence and moral progress. "As an independent nation," wrote Webster, "our honor requires us to have a system of our own, in language as well as government. Great

Britain, whose children we are, and whose language we speak, should no longer be our standard; for the taste of her writers is already corrupted, and her language on the decline. But if it were not so, she is at too great a distance to be our model, and to instruct us in the principles of our own tongue" (34).

Of course, Adam's and Webster's call for an official language was about more than national or cultural pride. It was also about politics and power. To establish a way of speech as more civilized was to deem other languages barbaric or less refined and to relegate speakers of those languages to the margins of society. In creating a language that was uniquely American, proponents sought to show the inherent inferiority of other languages and define them as inferior to the one they spoke. In the years following America's break from England, a series of movements were orchestrated to force Native Americans to adopt the English of White America, since this was supposed to be the language of a cultured and moral people. According to Jon Reyhner in his essay "Policies Toward American Indian Languages: A Historical Sketch," the American colonists "set out to civilize and Christianize the Indians, forcing them to accept Western civilization and to speak English" (41).

This, it seems clear, was about more than civilizing these indigenous people. In fact, Americans quickly found that the best way to pacify Indians and make them accept the loss of their lands was to make their culture—and their language—seem inferior. Formal education, which would teach them to abandon their language and "savage" way of life, was the key to solving what White people saw as the "Indian problem." This led J.D.C. Atkins, the federal commissioner of Indian affairs under Grover Cleveland, to declare that "the first step to be taken toward civilization, toward teaching the Indians the mischief and folly of continuing in their barbarous practices, is to teach them the English language" (51).

What can we learn from the linguistic actions taken by Adams, Webster, and others? To be sure, we must recognize the deep cultural and personal relevance of language. While most of us see it as a mode of communication, it is a window into our heritage and a reflection of our personality, and a way to wield power. When we tell a population of speakers that they are using "bad English" or that their dialect is not refined, we are making a statement about that community, one that is based on our perceptions of that community and their worth. Indeed, language issues far transcend any simple question of expression.

With these ideas in mind, it shouldn't be a surprise that Benjamin Franklin—another of our venerated founding fathers—also had strong opinions on the speech of people who were not like him or refused to espouse his political values. When Germans began to pour into Pennsylvania in the second half of the eighteenth century, Franklin assumed the alarmist voice that has come to be familiar among those who follow language controversies. Like others who fear the political power of a population that is united by language, Franklin decried the proliferation of schools in Pennsylvania and the notion that they might not adopt his language. Foremost in Franklin's mind, of course, was that the Germans would be more difficult to control if they were speaking a language other than English. "Why should Pennsylvania, founded by the English," wrote Franklin, "become a colony of Aliens, who will shortly be so numerous as to Germanize us instead of our Anglifying them, and will never adopt our language or customs, any more than they can acquire our complexion" (Crawford 37).

The more we study language and politics, the more we come to realize that much of the strife we see can be reduced to Franklin's trepidation about being "Germanized." It is no surprise that those who control language—through schools and books—also control people. Cultural power is promulgated and perpetuated through language and the values and mores that are embedded in them.

Franklin's consternation about the Germans and their power to resist English-speaking influence is no different than twenty-first century anxieties about Mexicans learning English or Black people speaking "good English." It is no different than the nineteenth-century agenda to make sure that Native Americans learned English and relinquished their "savage language." In each case, the person in power seeks to denigrate the opposition's language and persuade them that morality and social elevation reside in learning his ways with words. Thomas Jefferson, perhaps, our most celebrated founder, had this to say about the influx of Europeans. Again, as with other icons we have examined, notice how Jefferson's perception of a people's ethnicity is interwoven in his perception of their language. When we attack language, we attack the speakers of that particular way of communicating.

They will bring with them the principles of governments they leave, imbibed in their early youth; or, if able to throw them off, it will be in exchange for an unbounded licentiousness, passing, as usual, from one extreme to another. It would be a miracle were they to stop precisely at the point of temperate liberty. These principles, with their language, they will transmit to their children. In proportion to their numbers, they will share with us the legislation. They will infuse into it their spirit, warp and bias its directions, and render it a heterogenous, incoherent, distracted mass. (Crawford 39)

Language Is Personal and Communal

Studying language makes us quickly realize that it transcends simple communication. It is infused with pride and loyalty as well as anger and disdain. What we must understand when studying language is that diversity is a natural reflection of a culture's unique population, and, when we vilify a certain use of English, we are attacking the people who use it. Is it wrong and substandard to use a double negative and declare that "we ain't going nowhere until we fix this tire"?

Let's answer that question by first realizing that people have always worried about language and its proper or correct use. The reason, of course, is because language is intertwined with power. If a person can compel a population to admire his style of speech—and if he can per-suade others that his language is somehow superior—he can elevate his position above those around him. When William of Normandy invaded England in 1066 and defeated King Harold, he required that all official business be conducted in his native language of French. Both law and religion were done in the French or Latin language, and much of the subjugated population found themselves excluded from the activities of power. For the next four centuries, the English tolerated what *The Story of English* called a "linguistic apartheid: religion, law, science, literature were all conducted in language other than English, as words like felony, perjury, attorney, bailiff, and nobility testify" (73).

With the official language being French or Latin, the English -

speaking community was essentially excluded from the world of power. In effect, what they said didn't count because those in authority equated English with those who had been vanquished by superior forces. In fashionable and educated circles, those who wanted to have influence would speak in French or Latin, which was the discourse of politics and religion. English, in contrast, became the speech of the commoner. By simply opening one's mouth and speaking, a person could reveal much about himself and his prominence in society. Soon, French and Latin were regarded as superior languages and symbols of prestige. To speak French became a requirement for high society and social mobility. In the end, it became common knowledge that, as *The Story of English* noted, "Common men know no French" (76).

As we can see, language use and evaluation transcend any simple, non-political scenario. What happened to the English in 1066 is reflective of what happens every day to people who feel they either should not or cannot speak the language of power. And, as can be seen in the Norman invasion, the issue is not about what discourse is better but which one is being sponsored by those in authority. When people choose to speak a different dialect, they do so in an attempt to improve their self esteem, to bond with others who speak the same way, or to improve their chances for economic success. Speaking a certain way always carries risks. "It goes without saying," argues author James Baldwin, "that language is also a political instrument, means and proof of power. It is the most vivid and crucial key to identity: It reveals the private identity, and connects one with, or divorces one from, the larger public, or communal identity" (Delpit 68). Those who refuse to learn the dialect of power—or to use it in politically sensitive times—often become like Ralph Ellison's *Invisible Man*, who lived as an African American and endured the attacks of white people who saw him as inferior simply because of his race and the language he spoke. Gloria Anazaldua, a Hispanic writer, muses on her past life as a student and the shame she was made to feel because of her "broken" English. "So, if you really want to hurt me, talk badly about my language. Ethnic identity is twin skin to linguistic identity—I am my language. Until I can take pride in my language, I cannot take pride in myself" (Anzaldua 54).

People have always assigned value to certain dialects and languages, and such judgments have always been about their perception of the people using that dialect. Consider for a moment the Spanish language. As with English, Spanish speakers use a variety of dialects and some are imbued with more prestige than others. Some are seen as erudite and cosmopolitan while others are perceived as provincial and deficient. A Spanish teacher named Bernadette, who lived much of her life in Spanish-speaking nations, told me about dialect variation in the Spanish-speaking world and the value attached to different Spanish dialects. As expected, the people with the most tradition and power are seen as speakers of the best dialect. Many who speak Spanish try to approximate this dialect so as to be accepted into the social group these speakers represent. In the same way that a man will try to speak the Standard English of educated people while completing an interview, many Spanish speakers use dialects to enhance their chances of getting things done.

I met Bernadette in a Miami coffee house as she sipped coffee with friends who were both from Cuba and Argentina. "What Spanish nation speaks the best Spanish?" I asked the group as they enjoyed various drinks. Nora began by suggesting that the idea of quality Spanish is made in direct relation to its proximity to the language of Spain—the mother language from which its colonies grew. Nora and the others agreed that Castillian Spanish is the dialect that is invested with the most respect and prestige, since it is the dialect of the Spanish elite and reflects the speaking tones and diction of the educated and wealthy. Since Spain was the colonizer of other Spanish speaking regions—such as Mexico and Cuba—it holds a status as the oldest and most opulent of Spanish dialects. It is the mother language from which others originated and holds the same kind of special position as British English does for most Americans. Victor, a native of Argentina, added that he felt his country spoke a good dialect and that it was superior to dialects he heard in Miami or other parts of the Americas. Interestingly, all agreed that the worst Spanish was spoken in Puerto Rico, where the people spoke a "crude" form of Spanish. All agreed that their perceptions of dialect difference corresponded to their views of the people who use them.

When I polled four of my language classes and asked them what dialect of English mirrored the voice of the intelligent, sophisticated person, they overwhelmingly voted for British English as the most prestigious and English of the Southern person as being least educated.

Because it is the language of our mother country—and has historically been associated with refinement and erudition—it is given a special charm, an elevated status. For the same reasons, we impugn Southern English because of our collective memories of the Southern person in our culture. There is the redneck in "Smokey and the Bandit," the backward actions of Southern racists during desegregation, and the general image of Southerners as being clannish and poor. As Americans, we must never forget that language judgments have always been part of our lives and have acted to create solidarity as well as discrimination. It was through language that Americans made one of their first and most ardent campaigns for independence from Britain. When Noah Webster wrote an American spelling book in 1783, it became a symbol of America's burgeoning independent character and a chance for Americans to celebrate their distinctive ways with words. In setting up the first dictionary, Webster included many words that were specific to the rugged American experience. "America must be as independent in literature as she is in politics, as famous for arts as she is for arms," he wrote in 1783 in "A Declaration of Literary Independence" (181).

Much of the same pride and shame are true for speakers of other languages and help us to understand the caste system that exists in all language use. Gloria Anzaldua, the Chicana writer who we quoted earlier in this chapter, discusses the shame she was made to feel when speaking Spanish because it revealed her Mexican background. "Chicanas who grew up speaking Chicana Spanish have internalized the belief that we speak poor Spanish," writes Anzaldua. "It is illegitimate, a bastard language. And because we internalize how our language has been used against us by the dominant culture, we use our language differences against each other" (53).

What emerges from our discussion of language, thus far, is its incredibly dynamic presence in our lives. We are born with both a language and a dialect and learn very quickly that it is a badge of identity that marks us throughout our lives. At the same time, we become very adept at using language as a social tool. We switch registers or styles of speech to fit the social situation. We talk to our teacher in the formal tone she expects and walk into the hall to greet our friends in a dialect that unites us with them as peers. Throughout our lives we use language to become part of a certain language community, whether it is to get a promotion or forge a friendship. Language, in the end, is a tool for bonding and solidarity, for political gain and social acceptance. Efforts by political leaders to expunge certain languages from a nation are always unsuccessful since people see language as the glue that unites them, that best epitomizes them as a people.

Something To Consider

As you read this book and consider language and its place in your life, think about the different registers or styles of English you use in different situations. What were the specific constituencies that helped you to decide how you would speak? Did it have something to do with the power relations between you and the person with whom you spoke? If you walked into your boss's office and asked him for a raise, would you adopt the register that most fits his comfort level or would you address him as you would your family at home? Would you emulate the atmosphere of the last party you attended or would you be more sober and formal?

In dealing with students, I notice an interesting dynamic transpiring every day in how they manipulate language to fit the social and political context of the situation. While sitting in class, waiting for me to enter, they talk among themselves in a casual, informal register that fits their status as peers in an English class. When class begins, they quickly assume the formal, academic voice of students whose goal is to answer questions and earn a good grade from their instructor. As the semester transpires they become more comfortable with me. Their greetings to me become more friendly and open. They take chances in making our exchanges more personal, asking me if I had a chance to do anything besides read essays? In doing this, they strive to redefine our relationship and make it more of a friendship. Of course, we will never interact as true friends, but a certain level of trust is forged, which results in a different dialogue.

Such scenarios are common to all of our lives and help underline the notion that language use is context driven—that it depends upon the setting, the audience, the power of each participant, and the goals of the interaction. Most of my students leave class to speak to their closest social group in an intimate language register that is glaringly different from what they spoke in class. In the same way, most students employ a contrasting register with their lovers than with their platonic friends. Later, if they attend a sporting event, their use of language will again be altered by the expectations of the scene. In the end, what we learn about language is that it is dynamic and organic and living. If we are to be effective in using it, we must become astute at employing the appropriate register at the right time. We must become versatile linguists who switch styles to fit the context in which we find ourselves. Good English classes help students to practice language events by asking them to consider different audiences when writing a paper or giving a speech. This reflects the real world of language use, of language in action.

Language In Action

Consider the example of Paul and Marcus, two friends who meet periodically to play basketball in Marcus's driveway. Marcus is African-American and Paul is White and both speak a very distinct dialect while playing basketball together and when interacting with their families at home. Marcus's parents, both of whom are college-educated, speak an African-American dialect that is infused with aspects of the "Standard English" that is typically used by college-educated Americans. Marcus's parents reflect the influence of two very strong American voices—their family heritage and the professional register they employ when speaking as educated people to be respected.

As Marcus's father speaks to him about school, he is careful to articulate his words, to call Marcus by his full name, and to eschew any of the colloquialisms that are part of informal African American Vernacular English. Because he wants Marcus to appreciate the gravity of language, he does not permit any "hip-hop language" in their dialogues and expects Marcus to speak to him in a formal, almost professional tone. This continues until they are alone or playing a video game in the house. Then, Marcus is able to relate to his father on another level and enjoy the relaxed register that a son and father share. He is given more latitude with his father, but there is never any question as to who holds power when they have a verbal exchange. In demanding that he be addressed as an authority while in public, Marcus's father does not show shame for his linguistic roots but simply helps his son to see the importance of context to language use. There are different dialects and registers for different scenarios, and the sooner Marcus learns this, the better his life will be.

Earlier that day, Marcus's father had spoken on the phone to an old college friend, whom he had known since childhood. "You fixin' to hit that game later on," he said while preparing dinner. His use of an informal dialect—one that is clearly non-standard—reveals the comfort the two feel with each other, the friendship they possess, and the unnecessary use of polished language. Some of his most adorned and poetic language comes during these conversations and helps to highlight how competent we are as language users when we are not inhibited, when there is no fear of "power" being used to punish us for the way we speak. "He dogged that man—he dogged him and there ain't no other way to explain that," Marcus's father says with a silly laugh. It is the language of friends speaking in a tone that is devoid of any false pretenses, that is real and unvarnished. It is a register that is often not permitted in the English class despite its incredible potential, vigor, and validity as a way of speaking. Indeed, we do ourselves a disservice by not appreciating different registers and ways of speaking. All, in their own way, reveal fascinating things about our background and the relationship we have with the person we are addressing.

And what about Marcus and Paul as they interact in the driveway, playing basketball and talking? As the older of the two, Marcus rules the social context, while Paul aspires to be part of his friend's social circle. This includes abandoning Standard English and using as much of Marcus's African-American dialect as he can. When he misses an easy shot, he apologizes by saying "that's my bad" as he has heard Marcus and his friends say many times. Later, when Marcus accuses him of liking a girl in his class, he responds by dropping the verb and saying "Yeah, and you crazy, man." In many ways, Marcus has become Paul's mentor. Because Paul admires his older friend and aspires to be part of his social community, he tries to learn the language, to become part of the culture. This begins by adopting as much of the language as possible. In many ways, it is not unlike the Cuban who tries very hard to speak English so as to be accepted as a real American. It is part of the dynamic of language variety and an intriguing part of language study.

In discussing the use of dialect-switching, linguist John Baugh introduces us to the terms *hypercorrection* and *hypocorrection*. The act of hypercorrection is witnessed when a person speaking a non-standard dialect tries unsuccessfully to approximate the Standard English of his audience. The speaker is not successful because he hypercorrects and produces sentences and words that sound ridiculous and unnatural. When an African American who is not well-versed in Standard English tries to use it in a tense situation, he often overcompensates. A good example of this is fight promoter Don King, who appears clownish and amusing when he rattles off a series of erudite words that are often misplaced and inappropriate for the context. "We are here in the nation's capital to celebrate the coronation and adulation of the new monarch of boxing, one that has been venerated and regaled and revered with the accolades of his stature."

Hypocorrection, on the other hand, is when a White person like Paul tries to model an informal/slang African-American vernacular of his older peers. In doing this, mistakes are often made, which exposes the speaker as a fraud or pretender. In many cases, the speaker simply seems silly, as when I waited in line at a video store and listened to two white kids call themselves "dog" and ask each other "what up?" as if they were like some African Americans who use this vernacular. The dialogue seemed contrived to me but is emblematic of how people use language to consolidate social standing and establish themselves as certain social beings. Again, it is more productive for us to understand such actions and contemplate their meaning rather than to simply label them wrong or non-standard. As John Baugh reminds us, "linguistic variation does not exist in a social vacuum, and negative attitudes and stereotypes are essential components of discriminatory discourse" (72). Studies show that 80% of African Americans speak a non-standard dialect, often called Ebonics (Baugh 74), so, if we are to continue to treat it as something that is wrong or sloppy or simply not acceptable in any context, we are relegating many who use this dialect to the kind of alienation and oppression that the English experienced in 1066. What is the answer?

First, it is essential that we become linguistically literate and recognize the fact that we all speak a dialect and that none is intrinsically better than another, despite what we might think or hear from politicians or radio talk show hosts. In the same way that we all have a right to our own religion, we have a right to be respected in the dialect we bring to the classroom. This, of course, is not easy, since language is interwoven in politics and is never divorced from real-life expectations. While we have a right to our own language, we must remember that to be an effective communicator, we must accurately identify the appropriate language for the specific linguistic situation we are in. Language always has ramifications and meaning and is used either to exclude others or to create unity within a group. Noah Webster's American dictionary was a way of proclaiming independence from the British. The artist's intentional use of non-standard English is also a way of creating a niche for himself.

The Language Of Entertainment and The Arts

When we transcend simplistic notions about language, we come to realize how diverse and dynamic it always is. In no milieu is this more evident than in the world of entertainment. In looking at song lyrics we see a tapestry of dialects and neologisms being used in creative and surprising ways. Because they are artists, many singers and composers understand that rules of proper grammar are often broken to create a new and authentic sound, so lyrics reflect real people and are successful because they are so real.

Consider the lyrics of the popular 1960s song "Ain't Nothing Like the Real Thing, Baby," by Marvin Gaye and Tammi Terrell. In it, the singers use a series of phrases that are clearly not a part of the standard, academic English that would be used in a classroom, but the song is clearly a success on a variety of levels. First, the song touches on the genuine feeling that two people feel when they are in love and have lost all inhibitions, when they feel free to express themselves without pretense or facade. Second, it is the language—the true dialect—of the singers. In refusing to forsake their language, the singers are natural, authentic, and the song appeals to us because of it.

On a different level, The rock group The Police composed a song in 1980 simply titled "The Doo Doo Doo, the Daa Daa Daa." For the listener who wants proper English, the song clearly leaves much to be desired. The lyrics simply correspond to the singers' desires to make a sound that is bouncy and responds to the rhythms of the music. No, it doesn't make a profound intellectual statement, but it serves its purpose, which is to entertain.

Of course, music does use its creativity to make touching points about life. In Bob Seger's "Mainstreet," the singer talks in poignant lyrics about his life in Ann Arbor, Michigan and the solitary dancer he noticed in a bar as he peered in the windows. For the young Seger, the woman becomes a symbol of innocence, as she seems different from all of the other "hustlers and losers" he used to watch through the windows of the bar. "Unlike all the other ladies, she looked so young and sweet. As she made her way alone down that empty street/Down on Mainstreet," Seger says in admiring and romantic terms. The song ends with Seger reflecting back as an older, wiser person. The woman he admired from afar is gone, but her image still remains as a symbol of strength:

> And sometimes even now when I'm feeling lonely
> and beat
> I drift back in time and I find my feet
> Down on Mainstreet. . .

In composing this classic song, Seger breaks many of the rules of Standard English, and the lyrics could never be used for an academic report. It is not formal and depends a great deal on metaphor to carry a deeper meaning about his life and his ability to remain sane in a world that is complicated. When Seger says that he "finds his feet," he is speaking in metaphorical terms about feeling better about life by remembering his home and the memories that are embedded in childhood. Certainly, Seger could have elaborated on how a street could help him "find his feet" but most of us who listen to the song understand him and can relate to the special places that have good memories for us.

Seger could have also used other, more precise language to describe the girl. An English teacher might suggest that Seger is vague when he says she was this "long lovely dancer" and that he "loved to watch her do her stuff." What does he mean by "stuff"? What does he mean by "long"? And how does she "fill his sleep"? Clearly, the informality of his language is indicative of a nonstandard dialect, of people sitting around and speaking informally about life, sex, and memories. But then, this is the way Seger speaks, the way he thinks, and this is the most appropriate way for artists to tell stories in our pop culture world.

The inventiveness of his words radiate from his life. They are not owned by any academy of correct language. In essence, Seger—and other artists like him—are successful because they refuse to be stymied by the stiff rules of the English class. This is about freedom and personal expression, and it is clearly effective.

Again, we return to the word *appropriate*. Language is not right or wrong but appropriate or inappropriate for a certain context. Every speech event has particular expectations, and the entertainment world has extricated itself from most aspects of the world of Standard English. It is not appropriate there. As we use language and judge its efficacy, we must never forget the living aspect of language and its chameleon-like character in different contexts.

Perhaps, the most volatile subject in the entertainment industry today is the lyrics and sound of rap and hip-hop music. In its raw, unabashed look at urban life and the, sometimes, violent beliefs of its singers, rap has created a torrent of controversy. But what makes rap so popular is its independent rebelliousness—its refusal to speak like people who are different. When rap artist Nelly sings about "Pimp Juice" or "Dem Boyz," he is consciously violating the etiquette of Standard English in society and declaring his freedom from their rules. He is telling his audience that this is the way his community talks and he is not embarrassed to speak that way in his music. In doing this, Nelly empowers himself because he is refusing to be governed by the arbitrary standards of people who are not like him and who do not speak his dialect. In this way, Nelly highlights a second aspect of language—that it can be revolutionary or iconoclastic. It can symbolize the writer's personality and values.

The Right To Use One's Own Language

Perhaps the most empowering aspect of language is when it is used for personal expression and pride—when a writer can say I feel this way and I'm going to paint a panoramic view of those feelings, using my own colors, my own style, my own perspective. This movement to feel passion about one's own language should be respected in every language endeavor of which we are a part. The right to one's own language has been a struggle that has gone on for years but is still not understood by much of the American people. I want to look at two controversies concerning language and the law, so readers can appreciate the politics of language and the need to respect all languages people use.

First, we look at the Ann Arbor struggle, involving the schooling of young African Americans in the Ann Arbor, Michigan school district. This controversy began in the 1970s when it became clear that African-American students who did not use Standard English were being treated as learning disabled simply because of the dialect they spoke. Instead of incorporating their language into the curriculum and finding ways for them to learn Standard English as a second kind of English, many of the teachers treated the students' dialect as wrong and deficient and relegated the speakers to classes for those who had cognitive problems. The lawsuit which followed included testimony from linguists who educated the school as to the rule-governed, cultural beauty of Black English vernacular and the injustice in treating speakers of it like inferior language users. In the end, teachers were required to take classes in linguistics and understand that different does not equal inferior—that dialects are all equal in terms of communicative worth. In commenting on the Ann Arbor case, Ronald Woods reminds us:

> What many more of us need to appreciate is that there
> is a tendency, ranging from weak to strong, to view
> vernacular English speakers as less intellectually capable
> than their mainstream speaking or code-switching
> counterparts. This tendency is reflected in numerous subtle
> and not so subtle ways and can have a devastating
> though unintended impact on the child. (Woods 56-57)

The second controversy occurred in 1996 and involved the Oakland, California School District's endeavor to make Ebonics a separate language from the Standard English spoken by teachers and most educated Americans. Much of the political world was outraged by the idea that the talk of rappers could somehow be placed on a level with Shakespeare and Hemingway, but this response only reflected their ignorance about linguistics. First, most who vilified the Oakland resolution did not understand that African American English Vernacular (AAVE) is a rule-governed way of speaking and has the same components of any language or dialect that is spoken. Second, these same people did not recognize the alienation and shame that many have felt because language teachers historically failed to understand that dialects emanate from people's homes and echo the culture of their speakers. While it is unrealistic to forget about the politics of learning to speak Standard English, the Oakland school board demanded that people stop perceiving AAVE as some kind of anomaly, as some kind of sloppy form of English. They demanded that they be able to use Ebonics (a term coined as a dialect that many African Americans use) as a learning tool in helping flagging Black kids perform better in school. They asked those Whites that used Standard English to acknowledge the melody of languages and dialects that flow all around us and make our expression colorful. They, in the end, asked for respect. Lisa Delpit argues that "if students are to acquire a second language form in school, teachers must not only see their students as nondeficient, they must understand their brilliance, and the brilliance of their home language (42). Adds Geneva Smitherman,

> Ebonics is emphatically not broken English, nor sloppy speech. Nor is it merely "slang." Nor is it some bizarre form of language spoken by baggy-pants-wearing Black youth. Ebonics is a set of communication patterns and practices resulting from Africans appropriation and transformation of a foreign tongue during the African Holocaust. (19)

Of course, there are always risks involved in using language in unconventional ways. When Nelly raps about "Pimp Juice" or decides to spell "boys" as "boyz," he is alienating a community of people who are offended by a phrase that seems too far removed, too crass, and starkly different from its own dialect. Difference scares many people, and those who speak the majority language do not want to abdicate their power and privilege. When we study language and evaluate the words and sentences of others, we must balance their freedom to express themselves with the politics of language in the real world. If Nelly were to quit singing and apply for a job as a music teacher, he would adjust his speech to fit the formality of the speech act. This would be what is appropriate and what should govern our judgments about language use. At the same time, we must always strive to give writers and speakers as much freedom as we can, since language flourishes when it is unfettered by institutional pressures, when it flows passionately from the spirit of a person.

Descriptive vs. Prescriptive

Today linguists study language in descriptive rather than prescriptive ways. This is an important change for all of us who explore and use English. To examine language use in a descriptive way is to cease with monolithic caveats about how language should be used and supplant them with narratives about how different communities use and perceive language in their lives. According to Wilson, Dornan, and Rosen, a descriptive approach "describes how speakers actually use language rather than how someone thinks they should use language" (80). In essence, then, descriptive approaches consider the creative manifestations of speech and what they mean for a society, culture, or group of people. The descriptive linguist does not make hierarchical decisions about the intrinsic worth of someone's expression because the descriptive linguist holds to the view that all dialects have a place and are appropriate at a certain time and with a certain audience. Indeed, dialects do not spring by accident but are linguistic responses to social and political needs. And so, the descriptive grammarian would argue that there is clearly a time and place when double negatives are not only acceptable but preferable, especially if individuals are part of a family that use the double negative as part of their lives. The descriptive linguist celebrates the richness and inherent beauty of dialects, enumerating their history and the logic underlying their uses. Geneva Smitherman is a linguist who reflects this descriptive method. When she discusses the use of African American Vernacular English (AAVE), she highlights its rules, melodic sounds, and poetic qualities. No, AAVE is not the same as Standard English, but that makes it neither less effective nor acceptable. "Black youth bring a rich oral tradition, knowledge, and linguistic skills into the classroom. They are not starved for language and they are far from tabula rosa zombies in need of linguistic nourishment," argues Smitherman (159). For Smitherman and other descriptive grammarians, language variation is inevitable and a natural and welcome part of our communicative world.

American tradition is firmly rooted in prescriptive grammar and its practice of telling people the correct and incorrect way of saying or writing something and expunging unsavory dialects from their speech. In the world of the prescriptive grammarian, there is a right and wrong way to express something, and it is their job to inculcate the proper speech patterns in their students. For those who have read the many grammar books on the market and in classrooms, there is a good understanding of how unambiguous these works can be in delineating the rules of English and stressing the need to expunge ungrammatical constructions from one's writing and speech.

As I mentioned earlier, this is a time-honored tradition that goes back centuries and reflects our long-held belief that education should teach students to emulate the rich and powerful, to model their lives after the patrician class. The job of the language arts teacher was to give poor students a chance by helping them to be more like the upper class kids from the wealthier parts of town, to shed their "barbaric," uncultured ways with words and learn the polite English of the refined society. Sharon Crowley describes the typical teaching of language as "an attempt by those in authority to impose order on student discourse" (218).

Typical of this elitist mentality is William Mathew's *Words*, which was published in 1876. In it, Mathews discusses language in stark terms, referring to certain prescribed ways of speaking and writing as "faultless." The following quotation is symbolic of the prescriptive approach and its belief that there is a single correct way to use language and that deviations from that model are somehow less worthy or "pure."

> In language, as in the fine arts, there is but one way to
> attain to excellence, and that is by study of the most
> faultless model. As the air and manner of a gentleman
> can be acquired only by living constantly in good
> society, so grace and purity of expression must be attained
> by a familiar acquaintance with the standard authors. (338)

As can be expected, the legacy of prescriptive grammar has been a sad history of embarrassment and shame for those who did not use language in the way that Mathews and others approve. Of course, there is a

Standard English that we generally expect for many academic papers, but the prescriptive linguist goes too far when suggesting that there is something inherently pure or better about one dialect. Certainly, when we hear the Standard English spoken or written, we think of educated people, but that does not mean that this register of English is better— only that it is the desired register for formal scholastic situations. To make assertions about the people that speak a particular dialect is wrong and a sign of elitism and, perhaps, even racism or regionalism. Indeed, this elitism is applied by one people of one area of this country to another. This was alluded to earlier in this work. For example, sometimes, the Easterner looks down on anyone using some form of a Southern dialect. The problem of prescriptive linguists is they tend to apply a single rule to good English, teaching polite language in academic circles as the goal for all linguistic situations.

A Personal Example

I'll never forget the embarrassment I felt as a young college student when I excitedly told my philosophy professor that I was sure that I did "real good" on my exam. Of course, it was not the Standard English of the academy but the context seemed acceptable, since I had come to see my professor as a friend and thought the informal register would be acceptable. When he responded by correcting me and reminding me that "you mean you think you did very well on your exam," I felt an immediate estrangement from him. While he was technically correct in admonishing me for my use of English, he had sabotaged any chance for us to have a closer teacher-student relationship. As I look back on that event, I wonder who was actually correct. I was speaking as a friend and the fact that he did not recognize my informal expression seemed insensitive and pretentious—or maybe he was simply a prescriptive grammarian.

One of the ways we use language is to forge friendships and establish special relationships. When Paul sought to use the dialect of his friend Marcus, he was doing this as a way to position himself as part of Marcus's circle of friends. Language works in the same way as a special handshake or a certain style of dress. I was not surprised to see Paul wear the baggy jeans and sneakers that Marcus often wore. Language, like fashion, is a way of establishing solidarity and friendships.

In his essay "Ebonics: A Case History," Ernie Smith discusses the shame he was made to feel because of the Ebonics he spoke as a student. In the same way that Paul and Marcus use language to unite as friends, it seems clear that language is often used to create division and establish hierarchies of value. "Teachers and other school officials often used terms as *talking flat, sloven speech, corrupt speech, broken English, verbal cripple, verbally destitute, linguistically handicapped,* and *linguistically deprived,* to describe the language behavior of my Black classmates and me," he writes (17). For Smith, the failure of the school to accept or even acknowledge his language was a rejection of his family, his person, and his culture. The prescriptive approach that is so familiar in academic settings had no patience for Smith's natural affinity to his family's community dialect and made him feel like a pariah. "By the time I reached the ninth grade at Edison I was labeled antisocial and described as acting out" (18). Why was he unable to participate in the school's daily routines? Because like the students who chose to "diss" the system, Smith decided that he would reject the school that had so totally rejected him. "During my junior high school years, it was always my language competence or behavior that precipitated my negative experiences" (18).

The prescriptive approach to language has been the catalyst for much research on the validity of the speech minority groups employ. Researchers have delved into the speech of those African-American students that use Black English, studied their dialects, and concluded that their discourse—while different from their classmates that use Standard English—is logical, rule-governed, and utterly effective in communicating ideas. Despite what many ill-informed educators and language critics would have us believe, the dialect of these African Americans is every bit as legitimate and complicated as the dialect of any other social group. It is not the same, but different is not necessarily worse.

Perhaps, the most prominent advocate for this theory is William Labov, a professor of linguistics at the University of Pennsylvania. Through his life-long exploration of dialects, Labov has refuted the notion advanced by prescriptive writers that the discourse of Black children is somehow worse or inferior to others. "The concept of verbal deprivation has no basis in social reality. In fact," writes Labov, "Negro children in the urban ghetto receive a great deal of verbal stimulation, hear more well-formed sentences than middle class children, and participate fully in a highly verbal culture (Labov 153).

Labov was responding to a prescriptivist theory suggesting that minority children—and those from poorer or less educated families—are not subjected to the same kind of rich and thoughtful language stimulation that is generated in more educated homes. Much of this emanated from the work of British linguist Basil Bernstein, who argued that children from lower class homes speak in a "restricted code" while more affluent children speak an "elaborated code," resulting in more speech and more opportunities for expression. In Bernstein's view, an "elaborated code" produced more language use and more emphasis on accomplishing goals through language. The "restricted code," depended on a tacit understanding of social roles to get things done without the need for speech. Bernstein argued that these ways of speaking were governed by social relations within the home. If the relations were "open," the child was invited to be inventive with language and delve into novel speech forms. In contrast, if the home environment created a "closed system," children engaged in speech less often because they were relegated to certain roles within their family structure.

Bernstein never suggested that one code was inferior to the other but argued that students from a restricted setting would confront more challenges in school and other formal educational settings because their lives were simply less verbal and placed less emphasis on speech. A quotation from Bernstein might be helpful.

> If a speaker is oriented toward an elaborated code, then
> the code will facilitate the speaker in his attempts
> to make explicitly (verbally) his intentions. If a speaker
> is oriented toward a restricted code, then his code will
> not facilitate the verbal expansion of the speaker's intent. (31)

Something To Consider

I want you to do some descriptive language research and think for a moment about the way you switch registers (called code-switching) to fit certain social relationships in your life. We can learn a great deal about the social complexities of two people by analyzing the way their discourse is negotiated and the registers that are used. When people talk in careful and formal styles, it is often a sign that they are not comfortable with each other or that they have yet to decide which register is right for their situation. At the same time, we can glean much about who holds power in a relationship by listening to the conversation and the way people respond and the registers that are used. How do you talk to your boy or girlfriend? How does your register differ from the way you interact with your social friends? How has your diction or word choice changed as your relationship has become closer? Who controls dialogues when you converse? What can you learn from your answers to these questions?

Ways With Words

The problem with prescriptive linguistics can best be illustrated by looking at the work of Stanford professor Shirley Brice Heath in her book *Ways with Words*. What Professor Heath did in writing her book was to live among families in certain neighborhoods and observe the way they used language. Her mode of research was descriptive, in that she did not judge or correct the way these people spoke but simply learned from their practices and the meaning these practices had for their community. Heath chose to look at the communities of Roadville and Trackton, both of which are located in the Piedmont area of the southeastern United States. Roadville was a community of working-class Whites and Trackton an area of working class Black people. Both, Heath noticed, had very vibrant and interesting literacies, but neither of these literacies seemed congruent with what was expected from the educated people of the school, which resulted in a general feeling of alienation from both Trackton and Roadville kids. Heath's solution was to have teachers notice and respect their students' various ways with words and to help them incorporate their language habits into the school setting. It was critical that teachers understood that these working class people had different ways of formulating knowledge, articulating it, and making connections between school and community.

"In a sense," writes Heath, "students had to learn to code switch between systems so that they could make bridges between what they did at home and what was expected from language at school" (355). In doing this, it was critical that teachers respect their students' dialects and use them as stepping stones to the discourse expected at school. Rather than seeing different dialects as wrong, they saw them as modes of communicating that are effective at home but not always appropriate for school. There was a collaboration that acknowledged dialects as different but equal in terns of intrinsic worth. This descriptive approach was key to equality among all language users, no matter where they lived.

Doing Ethnographies

What Heath did in studying the families was called an ethnography. It is the kind of research often done by descriptive linguists because it allows them to observe and learn from different language users and reflect on the way language changes and how we can promote and respect diverse forms of literacy. It differs from prescriptive grammarians because it does not make monolithic rules about what is right and wrong. Instead, it describes language use and endeavors to understand its significance. An interesting way to end this chapter might be to do an informal ethnography. Look at your family and the way its members use language. How does it differ from other people and what social and cultural factors have influenced them? Does their ways with words work in school? Do these ways prevent them from feeling comfortable in a scholastic setting?

Democracy is a Greek word, meaning "power to the people." *Demo* is Greek for "people," and *cracy* is Greek for "power." If we are to have a true democracy in America, it seems clear that we must respect and understand the languages of all of our various students. Of course, that doesn't mean that it is acceptable to say "what up, dog," while beginning an important interview, but it does mean that we spend time learning the contexts in which such informal language is used. We all speak a dialect. We all understand that different language is used in different situations. The goal should be to practice different styles of language and learn about the rainbow of colors that adorn our linguistic nation. We all have a right to our own language.

Works Cited

Adams, John. "Proposal for an American Language Academy."
Language Loyalties. Ed. James Crawford Chicago: University of
Chicago Press, 1992: 31-33.

Anzaldua, Gloria. "How to Tame a Wild Tongue." *One Hundred
Great Essays*. Ed. Robert DiYanni. New York: Longman
Publishing, 2002: 48-59.

Atkins, J.D.C. "Barbarous Dialects Should Be Blotted Out."
Language Loyalties. Ed. James Crawford. Chicago: University of
Chicago, 1992: 47-50.

Baugh, John. *Out of the Mouths of Slaves*. Austin: University of
Texas Press, 1999.

Bernstein, Basil. "A Sociolinguistic Approach to Socialization with
Some Reference to Educability." *Language and Poverty*.
Ed. Frederick Williams. Chicago: Markham Publishing, 1970:
25-61.

Crawford, James. *Hold Your Tongue Bilingualism and the Politics
of English Only*. Reading, MA: Addison-Wesley
Publishing, 1992.

Crowley, Sharon. *Composition in the University*. Pittsburgh:
University of Pittsburgh Press, 1998.

Daniels, Harvey. *Famous Last Words*. Carbondale: Southern Illinois
University Press, 1983.

Delpit, Lisa. "What Should Teachers Do? Ebonics and Culturally
Responsive Instruction." *The Real Ebonics Debate*. Eds. Theresa
Perry and Lisa Delpit. Boston: Beacon Press, 1998: 17-28.

Fordham, Signithia. "Dissin the Standard: Ebonics as Guerilla Warfare
at Capital High." *Anthropology and Education Quarterly*. Spring
1999: 272-293.

Heath, Shirley Brice. *Ways with Words*. New York: Cambridge
University Press, 1983.

Joos, Martin. *The Five Clocks*. New York: Harcourt Brace, 1967.

Labov, William. "The Logic of Nonstandard English." *Language and
Poverty*. Ed. Frederick Williams. Chicago: Markham Publishing,
1970: 153-189.

Mathews, William. *Words: Their Use and Abuse.* Chicago: S. C. Griggs and Company, 1876.

Reyhner, Jon. "Policies Toward American Indian Languages: A Historical Sketch." *Language Loyalties.* Ed. James Crawford. Chicago: University of Chicago, 1992: 41-46.

Smitherman, Geneva. *Talkin that Talk.* New York: Routledge, 2000.

Webster, Noah. "A Declaration of Literary Independence." *Elements of Literature.* Ed. Sylvan Barnett. New York: Holt, Rineheart, and Wilson, 1989. 181.

Woods, Ronald. "Law, Ideology, and Social Perception: The King Decision and Other Language-Related Litigation." *Black English.* Ed. John Chambers. Ann Arbor: Karona Publishers, 1983: 56-70.

CHAPTER II

WORDS, VOCABULARY, AND YOU

Incident
Once, riding in old Baltimore
Heart-filled, head filled with glee
I saw a Baltimorean
Keep looking straight at me.

Now I was eight and very small
And he was not whit bigger
And so I smiled, but he poked out
His tongue, and called me "Nigger."

I saw the whole of Baltimore
From May until December
Of all the things that happened there
That's all that I remember.
                    —Countee Cullen

Words can hurt. They can even kill. Consider the significance of the word *Communism* during the McCarthy era, where one simple word could end a career, destroy a family, and even result in prison. Now, consider the term *terrorism* in our present time, where an entire nation has been embroiled in fear and debate since the attack on the World Trade Center. And finally consider the idea of *blackness* or *negro*. In addressing racism and the English language, actor Ossie Davis suggests that "the English language is my enemy. It is," Davis argues, "one of the primary carriers of racism from one person to another in our society." Through his indictment of words and racism Davis reflects on the meaning of whiteness and blackness in our linguistic world. While whiteness is overwhelmingly perceived in positive terms, blackness is consistently negative. "The word blackness has 120 synonyms, sixty of which are distinctly unfavorable, and none of them even mildly positive," argues Davis. "Any creature good or bad, white or black, Jew or gentile, who uses the English language for the purposes of communication is willing to force the Negro child into sixty ways to despise himself, and the white child, sixty ways to aid and abet him in the crime" (75). Truly, writer Aldous Huxley was right when he suggested that "words are indispensable but also can be fatal."

This chapter is about the significance of words and the need to appreciate them by learning more about their potential and power. It hopes to offer ideas for enhancing one's vocabulary while delineating the incredible power of language, of words, to fuel wars or create a poetic, song-like serenity. Words are symbols for what is most cherished and weapons for the most virulent hatred. Romeo was right when he lamented the violence started by the names Capulet and Montague and concluded by musing "a rose by any other name would smell as sweet." This chapter is about words—their power, their history, their mystery.

Our International Language

We all want to enhance our vocabulary, but few of us know where to start. Part of the problem lies in the incredible diversity of our language and its many influences. From Germanic roots, English has been transformed by invasions and altered by a long-held fascination with Greek and Latin. For four centuries, England was ruled by William of Normandy and his French-speaking subjects. As time passed, French and English began to interact and blend their languages. The English that existed before the invasion and occupation of William was now sprinkled with French words that would become part of its discourse. During this time, England was also greatly influenced by the Catholic Church and its ties to the Latin language. Those who wanted to participate in the holy mass—or read the holy books of the time—needed to know Latin or be estranged from the power of the church.

Throughout the centuries, our language has continued to change and reflect the political and social influences of its population. In 2003, when the French refused to join the United States in invading Iraq, some angry Americans suggested that french fries be renamed "Freedom Fries" as a way to show their indignation to the French. With the advance of technology, we see new computer terms enter our language. There are CDs, interfacing, downloads, hard copies, websites, and e-mails. Today there is *political spin* instead of *propaganda* and *bling-bling* instead of *money*. Each day that we speak the language, we unknowingly use French, Latin, Greek, and Native American terms and engage in reinventing the language through our innovative spirit. In many cases, we also use African-American words that emanate from the slavery era and have become part of our lexicon. "I'm so down with that," said a friend of mine recently. Twenty years ago, the same person might have said that he was "cool with it" or even feeling "groovy." Years before, he might have said that the situation was "flippin" enough to knock our socks off. "Don't even go there," said a student when I asked about her flagging attempt to be accepted to a competitive university. Ten years earlier, she might have simply asked me not to ask.

A Look At Joey's Language

Let's look at Joey for a moment. As our imaginary friend prepares for work, he considers the operation he will undergo later in the week. His orthopedic doctor has told him that he needs surgery on his foot, and it may require him to miss a few days of work. As Joey dresses, he is careful to put on his maize and blue tie, since these are the colors of his favorite college team, the University of Michigan. "You've got to be the most unorthodox person I know," says his wife as she gazes at his color scheme. "When are we going to the carnival?" she asks.

"I'm polychromatic," answers Joey with a grin, "but the jury is still out on how crazy I am. I need to rectify some problems at work. Let's go to the carnival after that."

In the short conversation we just witnessed, Joey and his wife used French, Latin, Greek, and Native American terms. They are typical of most English speakers who are unaware of how eclectic and diverse their language is or the origination of the words they use. All of us use the language of our speech community, but these communities change as we develop as people. Our first community is our family, and as we grow we embrace the discourse of our friends at school and later our colleagues in our chosen profession. Language is always a badge of identity, but our identity changes with our goals. From the carefully defined language of their parents, children enter school and adapt to their peers. Later, after years of using the discourse of their high school peers, they abandon it to enter new speech communities. Some go to college and are introduced to the polished language of their professors. Others enter the work world and must assimilate to the discourse of the employees. Language is a fluid endeavor that reflects our desire for power, identity, and accomplishing goals. "We speak of America as the melting pot," writes Paul Roberts, "but the speech communities of this continent are very far from having melted into one" (272).

Perhaps, the most edifying aspect of English is how it acts like a living person who changes to fit the dynamics of his/her environment. Words that had a certain meaning centuries ago, often reflect more modern ideas and values. And as our culture changes, our lexicon changes with it. Today, we give our population "props" for the "happening way" they move with the language. Years ago, we would have suggested that our population is doing a "bang-up" job of adjusting to language.

Joey, our teacher from the last paragraphs, is symbolic of how incredibly vigorous our vocabulary is. Joey doesn't know that *orthopedic* is a Greek word that unites *ortho*, meaning "straight," with *pedic*, meaning "child," since most children were patients of this kind of procedure. Joey is also unaware that the color *maize* is a Native American term that harks back to colonial days and refers to corn or that *polychromatic* is a Greek word that joins *many* (poly) with *colors* (chromatic). Finally, Joey is totally oblivious to the fact that *jury* is a French word that was incorporated into English during the time of William of Normandy or that *carnival* is a Latin term that refers to the festival of roasting an animal before the Lenten celebration. Truly, our language comes to us from many directions and is shaped by the needs of the people who use it.

Something To Think About

All of us belong to speech communities and share their ways of using words. According to linguist Paul Roberts, speech communities "are formed by many features: age, geography, education, occupation, social position. Young people speak differently from old people, Kansas differently from Virginians, Yale graduates differently from Dannemora graduates" (273-74). All speech communities are equally effective in accomplishing what the people who speak that register choose to do. Consider the speech communities to which you belong and how you feel about them. What do you do when you enter a different speech community? Do you alter your form of English or do you remain true to your speech patterns? Do you see another community as better than the ones to which you belong?

Shaping Words To Fit Current Values

The word *revolution* is a great example of how meanings change to fit the dynamism of society. The literal meaning of the word is to "twist" or "turn around" and is derived from the Latin verb *volvere*, which means "to roll." In our modern time, however, *revolution* has come to have a political significance that far transcends its Latin roots. To engage in a revolution is to overthrow a government, to depose a leader for ideological reasons. When the rock group, The Beatles sang of "Revolution" in the 1960s, it was in reaction to the upheaval in the United States and questions about the war in Vietnam. It is interesting to see how people in a society appropriate a word for their own devices and how these people change its meaning to fit their values and the trends of their speech community.

Evolution has the same root as *revolution*, and it, too, has a significance that far eclipses its Latin meaning of "turning." As I write this chapter, much of America is embroiled in a struggle over "evolution" in science classes and how the origin of life should be taught. Some groups that are religious want to offer a theory called "Intelligent Design" as an alternative to the notion that people evolved from lower beings. Whatever the answer, people will continue to take the literal meaning of words and use it to solve problems in their own lives. Words will continue to be malleable, elastic instruments for our social world.

Denotative and Connotative Meanings

Today, we understand the word *gay* in a completely different way from just a few decades ago. Anyone who has had the chance to watch classic movies knows that the word *gay* was a term to describe happiness or cheer, where today it is a label to describe an entire sexual orientation. Not only has the word's meaning changed in dramatic ways but so has its perception in society. This is the difference between denotative and connotative meanings. Denotative meanings correspond to the official meaning in the dictionary, while connotative meanings respond to the personal interpretations we give to emotional words. We all define words like *marriage, divorce, abortion, patriotism,* and *democracy* in different ways. While we can all agree that a marriage is the legal union of a man and woman, most of us disagree as to whether that right should be extended to gays or whether marriage is a positive institution. The same can be said for *abortion* or the entire issue of *choice.* People take words and use them to advance their agendas. Words never stand still but are used like musical instruments. Each time a person utters a sentence, she is reacting to the word's history and adding her own interpretation of the word to the language.

Some of us are Democrats and others are Republicans or Independents. Some of us might be Communists or Anarchists. In each case, these words are imbued with special meaning that far transcends the dictionary or denotative meaning. In modern times, the word *slavery* means something different than when it was used by our Founding Fathers. And, of course, our Founding Fathers had little notion of feminism, since they refused to give women the right to vote.

How Words Evolve

Let's look at the word *sophomore*, which comes from the Greek word *soph*, meaning "wise." Today, anyone who uses a word with *soph* in it must deal with the complicated way the word has changed meaning. To be "sophisticated" or "philosophical" is quite positive and suggests knowledge and a curious search for truth. However, to be *sophomoric* is to be pedantic, immature, and overly impressed with one's knowledge. Part of the discrepancy in the meanings can be attributed to the way society has changed the words. Originally, the Greek Sophists were wise teachers who were engaged in a search for truth. However, as time passed, their reputation changed and they came to be known for their deception, their artifice, and disingenuous behavior. Thus, in using the word *soph*, one must deal with the static dictionary definition and the dynamic way that people have attached new meanings to certain words with *soph* in them.

What emerges from our look at Latin and Greek words is how unwieldy they can be. Where we would like to be able to use roots, prefixes, and suffixes to define unfamiliar words, we must recognize that they are often not so simple—that society changes the literal meanings of words. "Every human language has been shaped by, and changes to meet, the needs of it speakers," (76) writes Harvey Daniels. Adds Jean Aitchison, "Continual language change is natural and inevitable, and is due to a combination of psycholinguistic and sociolinguistic factors" (439).

Consider the Greek word *eugenics*, which means "good genes." On the surface, this word would seem to be filled with positive meanings, but again we see society intruding and coloring the word in very pejorative ways. In the twentieth century, the eugenics movement, which began with animal husbandry, was used by the Nazis to eradicate Jews and create a master race. At the same time, many Americans championed a eugenics movement in America to stop disease and the breeding of less desirable racial and ethnic groups. In both cases, the campaigns were thoroughly racist and have forever changed our society's perception of the word. Today, *eugenics* stands as a totally contemptible word, despite the fact that it literally means "good birth" and other words with the same origin are also positive. *Euphony* means "good sound," a *eulogy* is a set of "good words," and a *euphemism* is a "positive expression" about something that is actually quite sad or deplorable.

Again, the lesson to be learned here is that words are organic—that they grow and change with the people who use them. While it is helpful to memorize roots and prefixes as a way to learn new words, we must appreciate the social aspect of language, the transitory nature of words. To know words is to be forever engaged in the study of language in the lives of real people, to see how words are bent and molded and formulated to fit our aesthetic tastes. Yesterday, I was insulted. Today, I am "dissed." In some parts of the country I prepare to go to college. In other areas, I am fixin' to go to school. Such word changes reflect the people who use them and sometimes these words become part of the mainstream. We need to be aware of the fluid aspect of our living language.

This is true of all words, whether they originate from Latin, Greek, French, or other places. While we are often told to study our Latin and Greek roots if we want to improve our vocabulary, it is often more difficult in reality, since people's perceptions of words change. In other cases, the words come from Latin or Greek and are too foreign for most of us to understand literally despite our knowledge of their use in our everyday lives. Have you ever heard of the word *ad hoc*? It is a Latin word and literally means "for this." It is often used to describe the formation of a committee for a particular goal. Another set of Latin terms that are used often but rarely understood literally are the words *de jure* and *de facto*. The word *de facto* means "from the facts" and *de jure* means "from the law." Often these words are used in opposition to each other. Either an action comes from an official law or emerges from actions in society. The Latin word *alter ego* is yet another example. While we have heard it often in conversations, its Latin meaning escapes us. In literal terms, the word means "other I" and has been used often to describe a part of our personality that often stays hidden or emerges infrequently. *Doctor Jeckyl and Mr. Hyde*, the novel by Robert Louis Stevenson, is an example from popular literature

A last example might help crystallize this point. Consider the prefix *para*, which is attached to many words we use on a daily basis. Learning the literal meaning of *para* might confuse more than clarify, since it has so many different definitions. In one case, *para* means "along side" as in *paralegal*, or *paramedic*. In another case, it means "beyond" as in the words *paranoia*, *paranormal*, and *paradox*.

Our pop culture is no different when it comes to words. The definition for a feeling or emotion can change as fast as the newest fashion trend. In studying words, we quickly learn that they are malleable, flexible instruments, used often to make statements. Think for a moment about the words used to describe approval. In the 1960s, it was not uncommon to hear some say "cool," "groovy," or even "hot." A decade earlier it might have been "keen" or "neato." Today, while often hearing the word *cool*, we are treated to a montage of new words. In a recent car commercial for Chrysler, singer Snoop Dog told his audience that "if the ride is more fly, you must buy." From "keen" and "groovy" to "tight" and "fly," our language moves to the rhythms of its users.

Something To Consider

Think about the language of our pop culture world and the way it has transformed our meanings for certain ideas. Would a fifty-year-old understand much of the language spoken by people on MTV? Is there anything we can learn from the change of words and how they are used to express ideas? Examine the lyrics of a song from the 1960s and compare it to one that was released in the last year or two. Any revelations in the linguistic change?

Political Language and The Words Of Propaganda

We use words to express our feelings and create a niche for ourselves. We also use words to manipulate and deceive, such as when political leaders choose certain emotional words to scare or inspire us to believe certain things. The 2003 War in Iraq made all Americans reconsider the words *terrorism*, *patriotism*, and *imperialism*. When the Bush administration chose to invade Iraq because it was supposed to pose an imminent threat to America, many wondered if the threat was real or if the president had manipulated information as a ruse for invading the oil-rich country. Within days of the invasion, America seemed to fall under a political chill as people were told that true patriots supported the war and their President. During this time, words became dangerous, as the popular group The Dixie Chicks were pilloried on the radio for simply stating their negative feelings about the war. Some wondered if certain words had become too risky to articulate while certain words were used constantly to create the right mental framework for war. Over and over, people were told about the weapons Saddam Hussein had and the dire threat he posed. Everyone seemed scared, since terrorists seemed to lurk around every corner. "One of the oldest tricks in the book," writes Mark Crispin Miller, "used against democracy or republicanism has been terrifying people, has been to create a crisis and to provoke a war. At that moment, sad to say, people often cease to become capable of reason" (206).

Fear, and the words that promote it, are perhaps the most cogent and insidious aspects of political language. Want to get something done? Simply scare Americans into believing that the alternative to your idea will result in disaster, lost lives, ruined economies. Consider the language of fear as it was used by George W. Bush and his cabinet in the promotion of war. Notice what all have in common:

> Saddam Hussein is a threat to America.
> —George W. Bush, November 2003

> The danger to our country is grave. The danger to our country is growing.
> —George W. Bush, September 2002

> We could not accept the grave danger of Saddam Hussein and his Allies turning weapons of mass destruction against our friends and allies.
> —Dick Cheney, October 2003

Three years later, we know that Hussein was not a threat to America and that the danger was not growing. But propaganda works on a visceral level to persuade us to do things we wouldn't do if we were thinking clearly. It uses key words. It plays on certain emotions. It creates an atmosphere that offers no alternatives and makes horrendous carnage seem benign. At its worst, it alters reality and deceives the people at whom it is aimed. And, of course, George W. Bush was not the first to use language to dupe the American people.

If we travel back in time to the Spanish-American War, we quickly realize that it was a conflict predicated on distortion, fabrications, and propaganda. Because it offered American corporations new lands for profit and exploitation, it was hyped by an incredible cascade of lies and exaggerations. Politicians and business people from all over the country told Americans that war against the Spanish was a noble endeavor, a patriotic duty. And yet, as we now know, none of the reasons for going to war were based on facts. Much of the violence in Cuba which led to the war was fabricated by writers simply because they knew a war would sell more newspapers. Newspaper owner Randolph Hearst ordered writers to manufacture tales of carnage and bloodshed, which resulted in the most incendiary—and completely bogus—tales of bloodshed against innocent people. It is perhaps the first American war that was based on mendacity and offers us much in terms of the power of words to whip up support for a violent and unnecessary conflict.

This, of course, is the essence of propaganda. It manipulates people to take actions when it is not in their best interests. Historian Leon Fink has called the last decades of the nineteenth century—and the words of the time—"the language of empire" because of the propaganda propagated about the inherent goodness of America's expansion. In essays and speeches, Americans were told that usurping land from the Indians was not immoral but an act of civilizing them. In colonizing Cuba, the Philippines, and other holdings of the Spanish empire, they were told that it was their destiny, their duty as great people to settle new lands and imbue the foreign savages with their greatness. Over and over, propagandists used words that equated attacking other lands with a celestial mission, with a moral charge. To advocate peace was to be cowardly, lazy, or un-American. Consider the language of Theodore Roosevelt in exhorting Americans to declare war against Spain:

> The timid man, the lazy man, the man who distrusts
> his country, the over-civilized man, who has lost the great
> fighting, masterful virtues, the ignorant man, and the
> man of dull mind whose soul is incapable of feeling the
> mighty life that thrills "stern men with empire in
> their brains"—all these shrink from seeing the nation
> undertake its new duties; shrink from seeing us build a

navy and an army adequate to our needs, shrink from
seeing us do our share of the world's work, by bringing order
out of chaos in the great, fair tropic islands from which the
valor of our soldiers and sailors has driven the Spanish
flag....(Roosevelt 8-9)

What does Roosevelt's propaganda share with the quotations of George W. Bush and his vice president? Can you draw conclusions about propaganda and its power to persuade? What emotions do both speakers evoke in urging people to support the war? What are the costs that are conveniently omitted? Before answering these questions, consider another speech from the "language of empire" and the words that stir its readers. Why is this language, composed by Indiana Senator Alfred Beveridge, also an example of propaganda?

Mr. President, the times call for candor. The Philippines
are ours forever, "territory belonging to the United States,"
as the Constitution calls them. And just beyond the Philippines are China's illimitable markets. We will not retreat
from either. We will not repudiate our duty in the archipe-
lago. We will not abandon our opportunity in the Orient.
We will not renounce our part in the mission of our race,
trustee under God, of the civilization of the world....
(Beveridge 270)

Something To Think About

Words are explosive. They can be used to spark action where none would otherwise be taken. They can inspire perceptions about life and survival that might not have previously existed. Look at the political language of Bush, Roosevelt, and Beveridge and discuss propaganda, how it operates on people, what it says and cleverly doesn't say.

Politics and The English Language

George Orwell's famous essay "Politics and the English Language" delves into the corruption of language and the nefarious ways that politicians use it to conceal their actions or to persuade their audience that their debauchery is actually justified. "In our time," Orwell writes, "political speech and writing are the defense of the indefensible" (564). Euphemisms are cobbled together to make massacres seem like defensive actions, as when governments kill innocent people and label it "pacification." Any atrocity can be made to sound tolerable if it is wrapped in the right linguistic package, such as when a population is forced by its oppressor to adapt its governmental practices and it is called "benevolent assimilation." Thus, adds Orwell, "political language has to consist largely of euphemism, question begging, and sheer cloudy vagueness" (564).

Official propaganda began in the early twentieth century and was the brainchild of George Creel, who worked with President Woodrow Wilson to establish the first official American propaganda machine known as the Committee on Public Information. In the early years before the war, it was used to foment a desire for war in the American people. Creel knew that most Americans were opposed to the war and that he would need an all-encompassing apparatus to stir fear of the enemy and love of nation. Creel's model—that words must be used dramatically as a way to lead Americans in a certain direction—has been adopted by other administrations and fueled the incredible consensus that Communism and other forms of government are evil, while America is a utopia-like place that must be protected through unwavering fealty. How is it done?

Propaganda seems always to blend doses of fear with a sprinkling of patriotism and guilt. Propagandists tell Americans that an evil other lurks in the shadows and it is their duty as Americans to vanquish this monster before it destroys the wonderful democracy they enjoy. In virtually every use of propaganda, the enemy is depicted as pernicious and evil and Americans are cajoled to fulfill their national duty, as loyal patriots have in the past. As a result, propaganda becomes a conflation of pep talk with melodramatic adventure. With the evil nemesis towering around us, we must come to the service of our nation and respond to our time-honored mission. Consider the words of Thomas Paine as he implores his fellow colonists to support the war against the British. Notice the language used, the tactics employed to touch his readers.

These are the times that try men's souls. The summer
soldier and the sunshine patriot will, in this crisis,
shrink from the service of their country; but he that
stands it now deserves the love and thanks of man
and woman. Tyranny, like hell, is not easily conquered;
yet we have this consolation with us, that the harder the
conflict, the more glorious the triumph. (94)

Now, take a moment to compare the statements by President
Harry S. Truman and President George W. Bush. Notice their similari-
ties and discuss the reasons why much of the propaganda to which we
are exposed sounds similar. Ruminate on the common elements that all
of the speakers share. What insights can you make?

One way is based upon the will of the majority, and
is distinguished by free institutions, representative
government, free elections, guarantees of personal liberty, freedom of speech and religion and freedom from
political repression. The second way of life is based upon
the will of a minority imposed upon the majority. It relies
upon terror and repression, a controlled press and radio,
fixed elections, and the suppression of personal freedom.
(Snow 58)

The American people need to know that we're facing a
different enemy than we have ever faced. This enemy
hides in shadows, and has no regard for human life.
This is an enemy who preys on innocent and unsuspecting
people, then runs for cover. But it won't be able to run
forever. This is an enemy that tries to hide. But it won't be
able to hide forever. This is an enemy that thinks its harbors
are safe. But they won't be safe forever. This enemy attacked
not just our people, but all freedom-loving people everywhere
in the world. The United States of America will use all
our resources to conquer this enemy. We will rally the world.
We will be patient, we will be focused, and we will be steadfast in our determination. This battle will take time and re-

solve. But make no mistake about it: we will win. (58)

In lamenting the mendacity of political language, Orwell suggests that "one has a curious feeling that one is not watching a live human being but some kind of dummy" (564). What Orwell is alluding to is the incredible uniformity that is evident when politicians try to whip up support for an offensive against another nation. Invariably, one finds the same kind of dramatic portrait of an evil enemy that looms ominously in the shadows and threatens to harm the speaker's audience. Fear is a powerful tool and political language often shares the same style of good vs. evil, of monolithic bad guys that defy reality. In many ways, it is modeled after the theatrics of the cinema, where the man in the white horse rides bravely into the fray and vanquishes the nemesis. "This reduced sense of consciousness," adds Orwell, "if not indispensable, is at any rate favorable to political conformity" (564). Nancy Snow adds to this argument by noting, "the propagandist strives for simplicity and vividness, coupled with speed and broad impact. He stimulates popular emotional drives. In doing so, he must for the most part bypass factual discussion and debate of any sort" (61). Perhaps the most compelling response to fear and propaganda comes from writer Michael Eric Dyson who laments, "I think the Bush administration has exploited the sense of terror generated by 9/11 for its own political advantage" (78).

When politicians are not scaring us or appealing to our strong sense of patriotism, they are using omission to separate us from words and the glaring truth those words reveal. We think of ourselves as a free nation that enjoys a liberated press. In fact, however, censorship has been a rather regular and sordid part of our national legacy. Perhaps the best book I have read on political censorship is Lewis Lapham's *Gag Rule*, which chronicles the long legacy of violent censorship in our nation and the way it subverted democracy. John Adams, our second president, was the first to make words dangerous, when he supported the Alien and Sedition Act in 1798. A person who wrote anything that could be construed as "false, scandalous, and malicious against the government of the United States, or President of the United States with intent to defame said government (or Congress or President) with intent to bring them into contempt or disrepute, or to excite against them the hatred of the good people of the United States" (Lapham 52) could be thrown in jail.

Such laws of censorship and intimidation were followed with Lincoln's suspension of habeus corpus during the Civil War, and the deportation of dissidents during the buildup to World War I. Woodrow Wilson, the man who ran on a slogan of democracy, was part of the Espionage Act, which criminalized any word that could undermine the defense of the nation. In recalling the ugliness of the era, Lapham discusses the fate of political leader Eugene Debs, who was sentenced to ten years in prison for making a speech critical of the United States. So too was Rose Pastor Stokes, the editor of the *Jewish Daily Review*, when she declared that she was for the people while the government was for the profiteers (64). "Nothing was to be said or read in America that cast doubt on the nobility of Wilson's goals, on the sublimity of his motives or the efficacy of his statecraft" (65). And, of course, one can never forget the terror and hysteria of the McCarthy era, in which millions were incarcerated or unemployed simply for refusing to pledge their allegiance to America and against Communism. According to Lapham, "between 1947 and 1954 no fewer than 6.6 million Americans fell into the nets of government investigations strung together with illegal wiretaps, false testimony, and synthetic evidence" (74).

Assignment

1.   Examine a political speech given by any U.S. President and be ready to discuss the language and strategies employed. Is it a style that couches truth in generalities? Does it create simplistic dichotomies of good and bad? Does it distort the situation to give advantage to the speaker?

2.   Write an essay on propaganda, exploring the language used and the reason why it works with people. Assess the damage done to democracy when society settles for this rather than substantive facts. Before you start, consider the logical fallacies listed below.

Bandwagon or Ad Populum: This is perhaps the most used strategy, since it persuades by making people believe that everyone is doing it, and they must become part of the movement. Because we are social beings and like to be accepted, there is a strong impetus to be part of the popular trend. Appeals to Americans as a special nation, tug at emotional strings but they also evoke strong desires to be part of the crowd.

False Dichotomy: The propaganda machine rarely neglects the chance to inject a false dichotomy into the discourse, especially since our culture is based on stories of good vs. evil, of good guys and bad guys. We are conditioned to see issues in black and white, so it is easy for politicians to paint a simplistic picture of the foreign boogey man that needs to be slain before order is realized. But is any political contest this clear and simple? Is everything black and white? Are there shades of gray that need to be considered? Many would argue that Americans fail to understand 9/11 because they have no knowledge of how brutal their own country has been in the Middle East. Because we do not know about our own acts of overthrowing governments and meddling in foreign affairs, we fail to appreciate the enmity felt by other people.

Appeals to Emotion: Both Presidents Bush and Truman used heavy doses of emotion in the excerpts we read. When we go to war because there is an enemy that hides in the shadows and has no regard for human life, as President Bush declared, we are basing our decision on pure emotion, upon fear of an unknown entity that could be anything. President Truman also mentioned terror, but never offered specifics. Appeals to emotion are predicated on an emotional rather measured response. Yes, we must always be wary of danger, but it is important to identify the enemy and use facts in making decisions about military actions. At the same time, we must know that most humans—even those against whom we fight—have regard for human life, love their children, and are morally invested in what they do.

Post Hoc Doubtful Cause: This is perhaps the most complicated fallacy to uncover, since it relies on deceptively cogent arguments for its case. An example of this is when a speaker suggests that America is more violent because prayer was taken out of school. To be viable as a premise, the assertion would need to show that rates of violence were low during decades when prayer was practiced and that a majority of kids actually prayed. The person would also have to show that violence and the cessation of prayer corresponded directly with a spike in violence. Finally, the person would need to explain why prayer makes people more quiescent or peaceful, especially since much of our religious heritage is rooted in violence.

Flattery: The language of the propagandists is filled with flattery for audience. The attack on another entity must be predicated on the notion that we are just and good and that our way of life is better than other's. In exterminating the Native Americans, politicians suggested that the settling of the West was a divine act that would benefit the world and that served the savage Indian. Thus, Americans were more willing to commit genocide when the movement was adorned in a language that made the conquest celestial. A great project for any language student would be to scrutinize the phrase "Manifest Destiny," which was coined by writer John O'Sullivan in 1845. In his essay, he suggests that it is the White American's destiny and even obligation to occupy the western land and displace the Native Americans. In many ways, he deifies the people to whom he writes.

Ad Hominem: This is Latin for "against the person" and refers to attacks that are personal rather than topical. When someone assails another's family or personal life—and those assertions are not germane to the issue—they are making ad hominem remarks.

Sapir/Whorf Hypothesis

The question that many ask in considering language and its relationship to certain people is how if affects behavior and perceptions. In other words, do we see women as being inferior because of the language we use for and about them? Another question involves the more general way that we think about our world and how language affects that thought. Those who study language should be aware of the Sapir/Whorf hypothesis, which argued that language determines thought. "Human beings do not live in the objective world alone, nor alone in the world of social activity as ordinarily understood, but are very much at the mercy of the particular language which has become the medium of expression for their society" Sapir argued (Fearing 50). Sapir was an American linguist and anthropologist who studied language differences and how those differences affected perceptions. Together with his student

Benjamin Lee Whorf, he formulated a theory on the relationship between thought and language. It seemed clear to them that a culture's linguistic habits affected its thought. The question that all of us in linguistics ask is to what extent our words and names and language structure influence our values and perceptions.

Sapir and Whorf's study of Native American languages suggested that Hopi Indians do not have a notion of time as English speakers do. The Hopi see it as a fluid process that cannot be fragmented into arbitrary episodes. But does this linguistic difference affect their ability to understand time? "In Whorf's view," argues Franklin Fearing, "linguistic patterns, operating unconsciously, play the dominant role in the enculturating process. These patterns determine how the individual in Western European culture analyzes reality. Other cultures arrive at equally convincing but quite different analysis" (53-54). Not only did Whorf believe that language affected thought but controlled it. Whorf believed that language acted dramatically but invisibly to diminish certain thoughts while establishing a reality for its thinkers. "Thinking," added Whorf, "follows a network of tracks laid down in a given language, an organization which may concentrate systematically upon certain phrases of reality, certain aspects of intelligence, and systematically discard others featured by other languages" (50).

What seems obvious is that language affects us and our views while being shaped by us and our aspirations. Harvey Daniels says it most elegantly when he states, "We make language more than language makes us" (78). As we can see in examining the myriad dialects and languages in our society, people are creative and enterprising when it comes to language. As their interests and values change, they find or invent new words to describe these interests and values. This does not mean that we are limited by words or concepts that we don't know. It means that language reflects the people who use it while it also helps determine their model for the world. This is why Noah Webster made a dictionary for Americans and why rap music is unabashed in using a diction that is particular to its culture and experience. Again, Harvey Daniels says it best when he argues that "every human language has been shaped by and changes to meet the needs of its speakers" (76).

Something To Think About

While languages are molded to fit the cultures that use them, they can also be used to move thought in certain directions. Words are powerful instruments and work to engender certain notions about people and events. Are women's lives and perceptions of themselves affected by our language? What about the language of political events? What about the language used by certain ethnic or racial groups? For decades, Black men were called "boy" as a way to diminish their stature and relegate them to an inferior position. Do you think the constant use of the word "boy" could have had an effect on their self esteem? When a woman is forever called "honey" or "darling," does she also respond to such condescending terms by seeing herself as inferior or impotent?

Assignment

Observe any speech act and consider the way language is used by speakers to control people and establish certain values. A political speech is a great idea, but so is a concert, a party, a sporting event, a dinner, or a meeting between a lawyer and a client. How do you talk to your teachers? Friends?

In Richard Wright's essay "Writing and Reading," the African-American writer discusses his discovery of literature and the way it stirred a range of emotions inside of him. For the first time, Wright could read others' stories and compare his plight as a Black man to the realism and naturalism he read in his books. As he reads, he realizes that words have incredible potency in affecting people. "This man was fighting, fighting with words. He was using words as a weapon, using them as one would use a club. Could words be weapons? Well, yes, for here they were" (789).

Clearly, words can equal power. They can be used to empower or emasculate, to include or dispossess. Toward the end of his story, Wright laments his inability to enter the world of literature that he has infiltrated. He knows no Blacks who read the books he likes and wonders if other Black people have felt what he experiences when he reads.

Certainly, Wright garners incredible joy from the literature he consumes, but he also is perplexed by the world of words and ideas. It is a power that he has trouble handling, this new universe of words that makes him restless.

Words can cause this kind of transformation. They can be weapons as well as vehicles for revelation. We can never forget the way words were used by Elizabeth Cady Stanton in her speech for women's suffrage at Seneca Falls, New York. In taking Thomas Jefferson's words and adding the word women to the famous declaration, Stanton highlighted the sexism that existed in American society. She exposed the nation's failure to include half of its population and made an incisive point about equality.

Learning Words

So how do we improve our vocabulary? As I tried to show earlier in this chapter, it is often difficult to use Latin and Greek roots to define words, since our vibrant society often imbues these words with meanings that are removed from their literal, denotative definitions. The word *carnival* is a good example. Few of us would realize that the word— which conjures up images of clowns, merry-go-rounds, and games—is actually related to the Latin root *carn*, which means "flesh." The carnival was the grand celebration before the religious Lenten period, so people customarily ate a lot of meat, since they abstained from such foods for much of the Lenten period. Today, most of us who use the word *carnival* have no idea that it is associated with meat, which would make this a hard word to uncover if we didn't already know what it meant.

So how do we increase our vocabulary? The first step is to make a concerted effort to incorporate new words into our lexicon and make them a part of our daily discourse. This is a gradual process that begins with the creation of word lists and continues with their use in our lives. I suggest that serious language students keep a journal and use new words in their daily writings. The only way to learn new words is to use them regularly. Simply memorizing them is not enough and will not make the words part of our permanent vocabulary. We must use them when we write and talk and hear them in conversation.

As a young college student, I gathered vocabulary words for a class I had and watched news programs that exposed me to higher level words. In watching these elevated shows, I was able to hear new words and understand how they were used. In viewing them and reading the newspaper, I would notice that words on my list were being used in print and on T.V. Soon, they became a regular part of my vocabulary and something I used with more confidence.

A final step in enhancing one's vocabulary is a study of Latin and Greek roots. As I pointed out earlier, many are challenging because of the distance between the connotative and denotative meaning, but that should not deter us from learning others. English is a mosaic of different languages, and Latin and Greek make up two of the largest parts. To have a firm grounding in these roots is helpful in improving our vocabulary.

Consider the root *mal* and its rather consistent use. *Mal* means "bad" and can be used to uncover words like *malevolent* (hatred), *malicious* (nasty), and *malnourished* (not nourished well). Can you think of any other words that are formed with *mal* as its root?

Other words are equally as revealing. *Poly* is a Greek word that means "many" and can be used to unravel words like the following:

>*Polyglot* (many languages)
>*Polygamous* (many marriages)
>*Polyphony* (many sounds)
>*Polychromatic* (many colors)
>*Polymer* (a chemical compound of more than two mole
>cules)

Another Latin term that yields many helpful answers is *bell*, which refers simply to "war." Consider the plethora of words you can recognize by understanding the meaning of *bell*. There are the following:

>*Belligerent* (combative)
>*Bellicose* (aggressive behavior)
>*Antebellum* (before the war)
>*Rebellion* (open opposition)

And there are more. *Pan* is a Greek word that means *"all."*

Consider the following words:

Pantheistic (all gods)
Pan American (all Americas)
Panopoly (all arms or dress)
Pandemonium (complete commotion)
Panoramic (complete view)
Pandemic (breakout over all people)

A final way to enhance one's vocabulary is by grouping or clustering key words as synonyms. This can help when we write and need variety in the words we choose. For instance, one might need an alternative to the common word *happy* or *content*. If you can find a few words that can be used as substitutes, you can add variety to your prose. *Happy* can be accentuated with words like e*uphoric, ecstatic, sanguine, blithe, content, optimistic, tranquil, serene, placid, joyful*, and *quiescent*. Not all of these words will stay with you, but it is nice to have words that work as synonyms, especially as you strive to vary your style and diction. Words are like beautiful flowers. They grow together and offer a slightly different nuance to your linguistic garden. But, like any precious plant, they must be nurtured and used—and shared.

Exercise A

Find creative synonyms for the following words and make a list for future language activities:

1. Intelligent
2. Cruel
3. Kind
4. Interesting
5. Strange
6. Thoughtful
7. Quick Tempered
8. Skillful
9. Sneaky
10. Energetic

Exercise B

Create words from the following roots:

1. Homo		6.	Di
2. Vor		7.	Acro
3. Sub		8.	Demo
4. Retro		9	Crat
5. Tri		10.	Mono

Works Cited

Aitchison, Jean. "Language Change: Progress or Decay." *Language*.
    Eds. Virginia P. Clark, Paul A. Eschholz, and Alfred F. Rosa
    New York: Bedford/ St. Martin's, 1998: 431-441.

Beveridge, Albert. "Albert Beveridge Defends U.S. Imperialism, 1900."
    Major Problems in the Gilded Age and the Progressive Era. Ed.
    Leon Fink. Boston: Houghton Mifflin, 2001: 270-272.

Bush, George W. Excerpts Taken from Nancy Snow. *Information War*.
    New York: Seven Stories Press, 2003: 58-59.

Daniels, Harvey. *Famous Last Words*. Carbondale: Southern Illinois
    University Press, 1983.

Davis, Ossie. "The Language of Racism." *Language in America*. Eds.
    Neil Postman, Charles Weingartner, and Terence P. Moran. New
    York: Bobbs Merrill, 1969: 73-82.

Dyson, Eric Michael. Personal Interview. *Hijacking Catastrophe*. Eds.
    Sut Jhally and Jeremy Earp. Northampton, MA: Olive Branch
    Press, 2003: 78-89.

Fearing, Franklin. *The Theories of Thought and Language*. Upper Saddle,
    NY: Prentice Hall, 2003.

Lapham, Lewis. *Gag Rule*. New York: The Penguin Press, 2004.

Miller, Mark Crispin. Personal Interview. *Hijacking Catastrophe*. Eds.
    Sut Jhally and Jeremy Earp: Northampton, Mass: Olive Branch
    Press: 202-216.

Orwell, George. "Politics and the English Language." *One Hundred Great
    Essays*. Ed. Robert DiYanni. New York: Longman, 2003: 555-
    568.

Paine, Thomas. "The Crisis." *Elements of Literature*. Ed. Sylvan
    Barnet.New York: Holt, Rinehart, and Winston, 1989: 94.

Roberts, Paul. "Speech Communities." *Language*. Eds. Virginia P. Clark,
    Paul A. Eschholz, and Alfred F. Rosa. New York: Beford/St.
    Martin's Press, 1998: 267-276

Roosevelt, Theodore. *The Strenuous Life: Essay and Addresses*. New York:
    Century, 1902: 1-9.

Snow, Nancy. *Information War*. New York: Seven Stories Press,
    2003.

Truman, Harry S. Taken from Nancy Snow's *Information War*. New York: Seven Stories Press, 2003:58-59.

Woolf, Virginia. "Professions for Women." *One Hundred Great Essays*. Ed. Robert DiYanni. New York: Penguin Books, 2002: 774-789.

Wright, Richard. "Writing and Reading." *One Hundred Great Essays*. Editor Robert DiYanni. New York: Longman, 2003: 780-794.

CHAPTER III

GENDER AND LANGUAGE

A woman reading *Glamour* is holding women-oriented mass culture
between her two hands.

—Wolf (70)

This chapter begins with a pop quiz involving the linguistic world of
men and women. While most of us believe that language is a neutral
medium that serves all genders equally, there are researchers who argue
that our public discourse—and much of our private communication—
are indicative of a sexist, unjust system. Is such a proposition plausible?
Is our everyday language a hidden device for gender discrimination?
Could something so common and pervasive as conversation be treacher-
ous and hurtful? Is author Dale Spender correct in contending that "No
more evidence is necessary to convince feminists that language is sexist.
What is needed now is an analysis of this sexism" (29).

Before answering, it is time to take our quiz. Your task is simple: Read the following magazine headlines and place them in the correct category. Are the following cover stories written for a male or female

magazine? The quiz begins in the next paragraph.

Holiday Drinking: The Professional's Guide

NASCAR '06. . . Get Set for the New Season of Our Most Ass-Hauling Sport

The Healing Power of Forgiveness

Fast Fixes for Misbehaving Hair

Start Eating Healthier with These Easy—and Yummy—Recipes

Hot Damn!

Few who take this short quiz fail to get 100%, since the language men and women use is actually much more different than what some of us might suspect. Indeed, in perusing the words of popular magazines—and in listening closely to a conversation between men and women—one finds that the language employed for and by women is dramatically different than that used for and by men. Consider the quotations above and think about the sharp divide that separates their meaning and the power that resides in a man's discourse. Would a man ever refer to his hair as "misbehaving" or to recipes as "yummy"? Would he refer to anything as "cute"? In the same way, most of us would be surprised or think it a bit unlady-like to hear a woman use the words "ass—hauling" or "hot-damn" in describing anything.

The fact is, language is a reflection of how men and women have been conditioned to behave and reinforces a reality that seems patently unfair. While men use language to please themselves and exult their sprawling sense of power, women use it as a way to be tentative, passive, and submissive. "Women are in a double bind when it comes to English," writes linguist Dennis Baron. "Words marked as feminine make women visible but do so in order to demean them" (190). Adds Julia Wood, "language reflects and sustains cultural views of masculinity and femininity. By defining classifying, and evaluating gender, language reinforces social views of men as the standard and women as marginal and men and masculinity as more valuable than women and femininity" (66).

Many will disagree, arguing that while men and women speak in different voices they do so with equality. Perhaps a man will say "Grab that spoon for me," while a woman will ask us "Could you please get the fork for me?" But such differences, many suggest, is simply a contrast in style. Neither is better and neither puts the other sex at a disadvantage. Students in my classes tend to perceive language as a democratic, inclusive instrument that is open to all on an equal basis, bending and turning to serve all people of any gender. They see language as an empowering vehicle for all genders to achieve their goals. As a male student said during a discussion, "My wife is very skilled at telling me to be quiet in a very feminine and forceful way."

Such reflections are humorous but fail to respond to a growing body of research that suggests that women are stymied by a language that has historically been unfair. Decades ago, writer Simone DeBeauvoir argued that women were subjugated as a population because their lives, their ideas, even their values were shaped by the men around them. In essence, DeBeauvoir suggested that women had no identity of their own, since they had always been defined and limited by their male masters. In her writing, she suggested women were always seen as "the other," as the inferior alternative to a man, the classic servant to her master, the one that lives to complement her better half. Such reflections are clearly supported by even a cursory glance of history—from Adam and Eve onward—as well as by the magazines in our own time. Where a man's magazine discusses what men can do for themselves, women's publications focus on men, solving their problems or worrying about their place in a woman's life.

Consider the following headlines from *Mademoiselle* a popular women's magazine:

How to find a Guy Who Will Really Love You

100 Men Reveal What Made Them Fall in Love with You

Why Nice Guys Buy Sex

Reading women's magazines quickly reveals a world paradigm that is consumed with men, making them happy, uncovering their behavior, and persuading them to love women. To read a woman's magazine is to be quickly aware of how important men are to women's lives. "Where are All of the Nice Guys?" asks another headline from *Mademoiselle*. Could you in any situation envision a men's magazine musing on the need for more "nice girls"?

And so, it seems that DeBeauvoir has a point when she suggests that "thus, humanity is male and man defines women not in herself but as relative to him" (54). This, of course can be proved with a quick glance at the way we label professions. For years, a woman was an actress, which was a way to distinguish her from a man, who is an actor. There is a patron and a patroness. There are barons and baronesses, princes and princesses, and, of course, a woman cannot be a king. In dozens of professions, women must become the alternative—usually the inferior alternative—to the established term used for a man. In the recent movie *Glory Road* (2006), the coach cajoles his players to perform at a higher level by telling them to stop playing like girls. Such characterizations pervade our language. Nobody wants to be a spinster, but being a bachelor is quite fun.

The Feminine Mystique

One of the most interesting arguments on sexism and language was done by feminist Betty Friedan in 1963. In her book *The Feminine Mystique*, Friedan argued that magazines and other forms of communication use language to create a subservient role for women. Even the most educated woman, she argued, is made to feel that her life should revolve around a man and be dedicated to domestic concerns. This stifling life, Friedan suggested, was the "feminine mystique" that was intentionally manufactured by publications as a way to keep women oppressed and less competitive. In her classic work, Friedan quotes from popular magazines of the post-war era and highlights their proclivity to prescribe passive, domestic roles for women, to remind women that they should be content in their ancillary, supportive role. The life of a woman, according to a long list of magazines and journals, was based on their ability to maintain a happy home, to appreciate the myriad appliances at their disposal, and to revel in the modern age of household technology. Writes Sheila Tobias:

> Sold to the American public by the media, by social
> and behavioral scientists and by sex-directed educators,
> this ideology caused women to be brainwashed into
> believing that success and happiness lay only in their
> traditional wife and mother roles and that the ad-
> venture of workforce participation during the war was
> a deviation from the norm (59).

Perhaps, Friedan's most poignant example comes in her analysis of "The Crisis in Woman's Identity" and her careful scrutiny of women as they realize how their lives have been limited and shaped by their culture's sexist mores. In doing this, she explores a woman's lack of a private image and the appropriation of her life by public standards. "It is my thesis," write Friedan, "that the core of the problem for women today is not sexual but a problem of identity—a stunting or evasion of growth that is perpetuated by the feminine mystique" (77). At the core of her argument is the notion that women are simply not granted the right to decide what path in life they want to take, not allowed to decide if a family and husband are the only way to fulfillment. Through publications of the day, women were being told that they didn't have the same rights as men and they were subverting their natural roles in life by aspiring to careers that were filled by men.

"Biologists have recently discovered a youth serum which, if fed to young caterpillars in the larvae state, will keep them from ever maturing into moths," writes Friedan. "They will live their lives as caterpillars." Then, she makes the comparison:

> The expectation of feminine fulfillment that are fed
> to women by magazines, television, movies, and books
> that popularize psychological half-truths, and by parents,
> teachers, and counselors who accept the feminine
> mystique, operate as a kind of youth serum, keeping
> most women in the state of sexual larvae. Preventing them
> from achieving the maturity of which they are capable. (77)

Something To Think About

An interesting paper could be composed on the relevance of *The Feminine Mystique* in our twenty-first century world. Some may say that Friedan's laments about an unequal society are no longer true, but others might disagree. Read the classic work by Betty Friedan and do a review on how germane it is to our modern culture.

Many would suggest that the "feminine mystique" Friedan delineates still flourishes today and is propagated by the various speech acts in our world. Whether it is a magazine, a conversation, or a book, one can see that gender is clearly addressed in the way women are treated or simply ignored. Again we return to magazines and explore the unique and very revealing world of women's language. Does such use of words and phrases—and the content of their discourse—restrict them and render them less powerful? Does it lead them to feel "emasculated?"

The July 2005 *Ladies' Home Journal* might offer some answers. On the cover is pop icon Madonna and the headlines promise "a soul-bearing interview about faith, marriage, and motherhood." One of the intriguing aspects of studying magazines is how graphics work to define men and women and foster our use of language. In this issue, Madonna is modestly dressed, looks pensive, and seems to offer her audience serious information about her life. The alternative, when gazing at a men's magazine, is quite stark. In countless works published for men, I found illustrations of women in seductive positions, seemingly posing for man's most lustful imagination. Whether one looks at *Esquire, GQ,* or the popular *Sports Illustrated* swimsuit issue, men love to gawk at scantily dressed women and use language as a way to induce them toward sex. "Do You Deserve a Hotter Girlfriend?" asks the February 2006 *Maxim.* This, of course, was preceded by the January 2006 edition that simply includes an article on "10 Maxim Guys Show Us Their Girlfriends."

The language of women is glaringly different. *The Ladies' Home Journal* asks women if they are "too tough" on themselves and offers advice on how to "Lift Your Spirits!" Another article addresses the question of sex but is clearly done in a way that is designed to please men. "Healthy, Sexy Skin All Summer Long" is the title. Another article in the Table of Contents features an informative piece on "Can This Marriage

Be Saved" and broaches the dilemma of a cheating husband. "While I was trying to get pregnant, he was having an affair," laments the author.

What themes or motifs can we cull from these uses of language? While this offers only a small sample of the publications circulating through our culture, it adheres to a pattern of language in which women are still entangled in the feminine mystique—in defining their success in terms of what they can do for men or how they can improve themselves for their male counterpart. The February 2005 edition of *Redbook*, another women's magazine, offers advice on "48 Love Secrets" and promises assistance on "seductive hair and make up tips." Hmm, would men ever read an article on how to improve their hair for women? In my examination of dozens of male-oriented magazines, I never found a single article on physical improvements that were designed to accentuate the wife's acceptance of the man. Yes, there are articles about seducing women and making intercourse more erotic, but all of these issues seem aimed at the male as a way to increase his pleasure and feeling of manliness.

Language again reveals interesting findings. In a feature about cooking in the *Redbook,* I noted earlier, Nigella Lawson, who is given the title "Domestic Goddess," is giving "tips on down-to-earth meals from the heart." And what is her most publicized piece of advice? "Men like simple food. Not fussy sauces or fancy restaurant fare, but good food cooked plainly" (23). Here the use of certain words seems very enlightening. The words "goddess," "fussy" and "heart" are words that are the domain of a woman and again reflect her less forceful lexicon. A man— not a real man anyway—would never cook "meals from the heart" or question "fussy sauces." To do so would immediately make one think he is "feminine" or even "gay." Sensitivity in language is the realm of women and language is consistently used to solve problems for men and family. It is the language of the woman and is how they have been conditioned to speak and write.

What other words are distinctly female? The March 2005 *Good Housekeeping* refers to "nagging pain" and offers a special feature on Kirstie Alley, the "sassy star" who has lost weight and who's "ready to make a big change." Inside, the table of contents offers more material on "dream hair," "Easter Elegance" and "six steps to the look you'll love" (7). Certain words stand out here as quintessentially female. Would you be surprised to hear a man talk about a part of his anatomy as "dreamy"? What about the word "sassy"? What about "elegance" or "nagging"? The 2006 issue of *Maxim* uses language to describe a feature this way: "Surprise! The Girl with the Hottest Body in Tennis." As one of my students perceptively noticed, "Women talk and write about love. Men write and talk about sex."

The Effects of Gendered Language

What is the result of sexist language? Clearly, this should be debated and researched, but many who study linguistics and women suggest that it has the effect of relegating women to an inferior status—similar to what DeBeauvoir argued earlier in this chapter. After years of reading magazines that direct them to beauty tips and home improvement— after years of being told that they should worry about cooking and lipstick—women are naturally inclined to believe that their place lies in issues that are trivial and designed to please the opposite sex— inclined to see themselves as ancillary. "Women are deeply affected by what their magazines tell them," writes Naomi Wolf, "because they are all most women have as a window on their mass sensibility" (70).

In her book *Talking from 9-5*, linguist Deborah Tannen contends that a woman's language is inherently passive, apologetic, and tentative. While men speak with aggressive authority and interrupt their female counterparts, women blithely sit in the shadows and say they're sorry for incidents that are not even their fault. Their language has placed them in a context of fealty, and they are programmed to play their part. While men spar and debate, women seek resolution and inclusion. "Conversational rituals common to men often involve using opposition such as banter, joking, teasing, and playful put-downs, and expending effort to avoid the one-down position in the interaction," (23) writes Tannen. "Conversational rituals among women," in contrast, "are often ways of maintaining appearance of equality, taking into account the effect of the exchange on the other person, and expending effort to downplay the speaker's authority so they can get the job done without flexing their muscles in an obvious way" (23).

In short, it seems that power seems embedded in the language of men, while women use the language of the peacemaker, the soft, sassy, and less important person. Some might suggest that a language that employs words like "sassy" and "divine" will not be taken seriously in a professional competitive world. Some would further argue that such language is the catalyst for female oppression and misogyny. It is a convenient and almost invisible way to see women as a diminished version of a man. Indeed, the language women employ seems intertwined in caring for a man and solving their problems as a couple. And, in the end, how can one both worry and compete against a person for a career?

Tannen also points to the consistently aggressive demeanor of men's language. In studying interactions, Tannen found that women apologize as a conversational ritual and unwittingly place themselves in a subordinate position when doing so. "Admitting fault can be explained as taking a one-down position. When both parties take the blame, they end up on an equal footing" (46). What was revealing for Tannen was the way men eschewed the apology while women did it even when there was no reason for it. She further argues that men engage in "ritual fighting" as a way to sharpen their rhetorical skills while women are more likely to appease and comply, to capitulate to the ardent arguments of their male counterpart.

As a whole, women are conditioned to be less aggressive with language, to use it more to solve problems while men use it to construct a plan that exults their expertise and mastery of an issue. "Women are more likely to downplay their certainty" while "men are more likely to downplay their doubts," (35-36) adds Tannen.

What emerges from the various anecdotes in *Talking from 9-5* is a collection of humorous and sometimes disconcerting examples of how women in the workplace sabotage their success because of the language they have learned to use. In the end, Tannen concludes by wondering if the language women employ is sufficient for those who aspire to be successful professionals. "How you talk creates power," writes Tannen in her final chapter, and the ritual of conversation must be learned if we are to understand ourselves and the way our language influences and subverts women and their careers.

Much of the research seems to support Tannen, especially as it relates to the way men and women speak. For instance, there seems to be a general agreement among experts that women talk in an "expressive" style while men employ an "instrumental" mode of communication. To be expressive, one tends to reveal more emotion and offer compassion to the listener. In contrast, an instrumental style is grounded in assertiveness and power. Men who use instrumental communication tend to do it as a way to prove or establish their status. Again, linguist Julia Woods captures the differences when she argues "masculine speech communities tend to regard talk as a way to exert control, preserve independence, entertain, and enhance status. Conversation is often seen as an arena for proving oneself and negotiating prestige" (61).

What's In A Name?

Much of the subjugation we see in a woman's discourse might be based on the words and names we have historically used for men and women. Again, much of this works on a subconscious level but remains a potent vehicle in driving each gender to see their counterpart in a certain way. Linguist Alleen Pace Nilsen has done interesting research on the language of sexism, with particular attention to the names ascribed to women. She suggests that names offer a prism into our views of men and our androcentric worldview. "The names that people give their children show the hopes and dreams they have for them, and when we look at the differences between male and female names in our culture we can see the cumulative expectations of that culture," muses Nilsen (307).

And what names—and expectations—do we honor our women with? First, Nilsen notes that we seem to think of women in terms of pretty but rather staid and passive ornaments. We name our girls after flowers, like *Rose, Daisy, Violet, Myrtle, Heather, Iris,* and *Ivy.* If girls are not wavering plants in the cold wind, they are precious possessions, such as when we name them *Pearl, Jewel, Ruby, Crystal,* or *Ada,* which means "ornament." Is *April* named after the month because of its array of arboreal splendor? Is *June* a woman's name because it evokes images of a pleasant day in the sun, surrounded by a tapestry of green grass and colorful flowers? What about *Autumn* and *Spring,* which are popular names for girls? Whatever the answer, it seems clear that women live with names that position them in a weak, pretty, or innocuously pleasant context.

Compare these rather harmless and pretty names to those we give men. *Neil* means "champion," *Raymond* means "wise protection,"

Richard is "strong king," and *Rex* means "king." For those who think about the meanings of names and their relevance to people who are given them, it becomes a little disquieting to know that *Vanessa*, meaning "butterfly," could someday marry and try to be equal with *Harold*, whose name means "chief of the army." Indeed, the more we delve into the language, the more revealing and troubling it is. The word *virile*, which means "man" also refers to virtue and honor. The comparison to this would be *hysterical*, which means "emotionally unstable" and refers exclusively to a woman's anatomy and her tendency to be irascible because of her biology. "Language is like an X-ray in providing visible evidence of invisible thoughts," writes Nilsen (309) toward the end of her work. If this is true, what does our X-ray of names reveal about gender and equality?

Something To Think About

Continue our search for names and write a paper about the significance of names and how they affect our culture and views of each other. A male Native American was traditionally called a *Brave* while a woman was a *Squaw*. A husband is the Master of the family, while the woman is the *cute chick*, *hot babe*, or *vixen* that he married. The fact that women forfeit their name and take their husband's seems incredibly anachronistic in our modern world, especially since it was a sign that the woman now was property that belonged to her husband. Do you believe that names and their associations to certain meanings have a critical effect on our view of people? Do you think that gender is profoundly affected by the language that courses through it? Argue for your conclusion.

What Literature Hides

One of the most troubling aspects of language and gender is the realization that much of the writing done by women has been ignored or trivialized simply because the author was female. In her classic book *Sensational Designs*, Jane Tompkins argues that many of the great writers of the nineteenth century were marginalized and disposed of because of the political machinations of powerful men. A good example of this is

Harriet Beecher Stowe and her wildly popular nineteenth century novel *Uncle Tom's Cabin.* While it was much more widely read than *The Adventures of Huckleberry Finn*—and was much more influential in affecting the Civil War—Stowe's novel was treated with condescension by later scholars, who assessed its literary value as less powerful simply because it was written by a woman and considered too "romantic" or sentimental for serious literature.

According to Tompkins, *Uncle Tom's Cabin* was "in almost any terms one can think of, the most important book of the century" (124). And yet, because it was considered a woman's novel or a sentimental piece of writing, its incredible popularity was minimized by later critics who read it. Tompkins argues cogently for acceptance of the sentimental novel and decries the attitude of male critics who dismiss it simply because it does not appeal to male ideas of literature. "We can and should set aside the modernist prejudices that consign this fiction to oblivion, in order to see how it worked for its readers, in its time, with such unexampled effect," argues Tompkins (127).

Ignoring women has resulted in what Tompkins calls "The Other American Renaissance," where women wrote books and moved their audiences but were later expunged from the pantheon of great works because of misogyny. Today, we read about Melville, Hawthorne, Thoreau, Emerson, Twain, and Whitman, but fail to acknowledge the fact that there was a cadre of women who were much more successful than these much-exulted male writers. Besides Stowe, who wrote a novel that galvanized an entire nation to war, there was Susanne Warner's *The Wide, Wide World*, written in 1850 and unprecedented in its national appeal. What these novels had in common is their popularity for both men and women. While they did have moments of melodrama and were crafted in a didactic manner, they were emblematic of the national psyche at the time. Why, many wonder, were the hundreds of female works ignored or buried by critics of later years, when they flourished in their own era?

Perhaps, the answer lies in the incredible power of language. For those who are muted, there is little hope to effect change. While language does not control us, it certainly affects our perception of people and actions. This is why African Americans no longer want to be called *colored* and why hunters hide their blood sport in a word like *harvesting.*

It is why gambling is now labeled *gaming* and why women do not want to be called *girls*. Today, one does not buy a used car but one that is *pre-owned*, suggesting that it was bought but never actually driven. Clearly, language affects our perceptions and reflects our desire to deceive and manipulate through words that are used and those that are omitted. And when we have no stories to present our experience of the world—as we see in the dearth of female literature—we begin to appreciate the power of language to discriminate and exclude. Again, we think of Ellison's *Invisible Man* and his lament that he was simply never seen, that he failed to exist for the white people in his world. This is the same way that Virginia Woolf felt when she questioned "what is a woman" and declared that she did not know. "I do not believe that anybody can know until she has expressed herself in all the arts and professions open to human skill" (777).

In the essay "Women and Literary History," Dale Spender suggests that the disappearance of women's literature is not a mistake but part of a concerted effort to maintain a male-oriented literary canon. "The decision-making powers were concentrated in the hands of men who not surprisingly found the good and the great among their fellow men," (21) writes Spender. And so, after years of being successful writers in their own time, female writers were excluded from publications that would assure them fame in future generations. "I have been able to find one hundred good women novelists of the eighteenth century and together they were responsible for almost six hundred novels," writes Spender. And yet, she adds, they have all disappeared" (18).

Is this because these writers simply were not accorded professional recognition in their own time? Clearly, adds Spender, this is not the case. In fact, Spender adds, women writers were the majority in their time. They were the esteemed majority. "They were highly praised by readers and reviewers alike. They were valued by some of the best educated and most distinguished persons—of both sexes" (20). And yet, today they have disappeared or linger on the fringes of reading lists because they were ignored by powerful editors and publishers who seemed unwilling to give them the success they earned in their own time. Language, it seems clear, can be used as a weapon or as a way to silence those who seek a voice. "To speak and to write publicly is to threaten the patriarchal order," write Spender in the book *Man Made*

Language. This is why it is important to control language and to consign certain people to limited kinds of discourse. It is why American governments have practiced subtle kinds of censorship, by suggesting that certain kinds of writing were subversive or obscene.

Censorship and The Comstock Law

In the nineteenth century, Americans were prevented from getting any information that involved sexual liberation or birth control under what was known as the Comstock Law. Not only did the law exclude literature about birth control or sexual education but also made it illegal to disseminate literature about safe and reliable ways to limit one's family. During this time, women were arrested simply for commiserating about the travails of having children and the need for safe alternatives. Speakers were condemned and threatened. Meetings were disrupted. Publishers of newsletters on ways to stop pregnancies were told to desist or face incarceration. Clearly, as Margaret Sanger and other crusaders of the time realized, language and the education it offers is dangerous and must be controlled by those in power.

Something To Think About

Women were told that serious writing was beyond their ken and often had to resort to changing their names in order to have their work published. George Eliot is a perfect example. Who is George Eliot? She is actually Marianne Evans, the author of such nineteenth century classics as *The Mill on the Floss*. Eliot changed her name because professional writing was closed to women. Men knew that language was imbued with power and wanted to exclude women. In fact, history shows us that there have been concerted campaigns over the years to prevent disaffected groups—especially women—from learning to write. While reading was considered safer—since it usually involved the Bible and static, masculine interpretations of its "truths"—writing was often seen as subversive and disputatious.

Deborah Brandt discusses the trepidation many religious groups felt when the poor began to learn to write. She cites an attempt by the Wesleyan Methodist Conference to prevent people from learning to write in their Sunday schools. The fear was that the students would use writing for power, that literacy would become more than a way to reinforce obedience. "Unlike reading, with its direct and traditional connection to piety and Bible study, writing was considered too secular, worldly, and vocational and too strongly associated with upward mobility" (146). In short, literacy can be used to hinder or stir power. We can use it to prevent women from being creatively independent beings or employ it to unleash the individual in all people. The fact that women have been carefully limited in their literacy learning tells us much about the potential of words to transform the world.

Women and The Bible

> It is sad but true that decisions in such important matters as the language in which we worship, the language of catechesis and even language of sacred scripture has been heavily influenced by organized pressure groups dedicated to the agenda of militant feminism. (St Joseph Foundation Staff and Friends)

This chapter concludes with a short look at a revealing controversy concerning gender, language, and the Bible. It seems that various religious organizations have been in a simmering debate about the correct or proper use of gender in Biblical language. "One of the most controversial features of several recent versions of the Bible has been the use of gender-neutral language," writes Michael D. Marlowe in his online article. "Many articles and at least three books have appeared dealing with this issue in the past seven years" (The Gender Neutral Controversy).

Specifically, the issue revolves around the notion that all Biblical references to man should be changed so that they include women or become gender-neutral. While many agree that it is time to revise the Bible and expunge sexist, exclusionary passages from the text, others worry that such revisions and selective editing will subvert the Bible's sacred message. "Gender-neutral" language seeks to eliminate references to men when it is clear that the writer's subject was all people, so that society or all people are not limited by a word like "man." Other coalitions seek to completely expunge the word "man" from the Bible—even in reference to God.

Of course, we must remember that our language has long been managed by men and the Bible is clearly a reflection of what has come to be called a "patriarchal society." The Old Testament depicts Hebrew women as chattel, unable to make decisions or serve man as anything more than a helper and bearer of children. It clearly supports the notion of women as a physical possession, and it is no mistake that Abraham was invited to have sex with his servant Hagar when Sara was unable to give him a child. Such an act was permissible if a man's wife was unable to give him children, as it was assumed that the woman had failed in her duty. In Genesis, when God sends Adam out of the Garden of Eden, he omits any mention of Eve, and in Exodus, God is described as "the God of Abraham, Isaac, and Jacob" with no mention of their wives. And, of course, Lot is happy to offer his two daughters to the lustful crowd to protect the male angels who are visiting him in the story of Sodom and Gomorrah.

To be inclusive is to make women a part of the Biblical story— to replace the androcentric aspects of the Bible with modern versions that stop assuming that women are simply appendages of their husbands or fathers. In some cases this seems sensible while in others it creates a more awkward reading that has stirred controversy in many churches. In addition, many conservative or evangelical Christians reject the idea of changing the Bible simply to appease feminists. They worry that the Bible will capitulate to political pressure and become an artifact that is more popular than accurate. In her article "Femme Fatale," Susan Olasky refers to the movement in apocalyptic terms, suggesting that the movement to include women in the Bible's language amounts to a "feminist seduction of the evangelical church" (2).

In making her argument, Olasky contends that holy passages would become less accurate because they are made gender neutral. In some cases, the word *man* would be replaced with a plural pronoun, such as when "Blessed is the man who walks not in the counsel of the wicked, nor stands in the way of sinners...but his delight is in the law of the Lord" is changed to "Happy are those who do not follow the advice of the wicked...but their delight is in the law of the Lord." Is this a change that compromises or sullies the holy meaning of the passage? Is gender inclusion making the Bible better or simply much different?

In another passage, "Let us make man in our image" would be changed to "Let us make humankind in our image." While this makes the passage less stylistically pleasing, it does reflect the notion that women were considered part of God's plan. Problems also surface, as attempts are made to expunge any masculine pronouns from the language. Critics point to Galatians 6:7 (KJV) where Paul wrote, "Whatever a man sows, that will he also reap." This is replaced with the words, "Whatever a person sows, that person will also reap." In Genesis, the gender inclusive version man is again supplanted with humankind in the well-known phrase "so God created humankind in his image."

Whatever happens in the future, one thing seems clear: Language makes a difference because those who control language have power to direct and even create reality. Indeed, one of the most spirited fights among conservatives and feminists has revolved around the gender of God. Some want to eliminate sex from the Creator's essence, while others maintain God's male persona. Why, we need to ask ourselves, is this important? What are the implications of a gendered God and why can't God be devoid of gender, especially since he is a God for all living beings on earth? Perhaps, our language and the titles and words we give to people—and those we omit—have more influence on our society than we first thought. Perhaps, our language does alter our perceptions of the world. Perhaps words and titles are germane to our reality. Whatever the answer, it is clear that language is an incendiary issue that inflames the emotions of the most prominent leaders. If it didn't, major religious leaders would not fight to have the gendered language either changed or maintained in its present form. Clearly, our language has an impact on our genders and the way we see ourselves.

Works Cited

Baron, Dennis. *Grammar and Gender*. New Haven: Yale University Press, 1987.

Brandt, Deborah. *Literacy in American Lives*. New York: Cambridge University Press, 2001.

DeBeauvoir, Simone. "Woman as Other." *The Gender Reader*. Eds. Evelyn Ashton-Jones, Gary A. Olson, and Merry G. Perry. Boston: Allyn and Bacon, 2000: 53-59.

Friedan, Betty. *The Feminine Mystique*. New York: W.W. Norton and Company, 1997.

King James Version, 3rd edition. New York: Ransom Religious Press, 2005.

Marlowe, Michael D. "The Gender Neutral Controversy." Jan. 2005. 27 July 2006 <www.bible-research.com>.

Nilsen, Alleen Pace. "Sexism in English: A 1990s Update." *The Gender Reader*. Eds. Evelyn Ashton-Jones, Gary A. Olson, and Merry G. Perry. Boston: Allyn and Bacon, 2000: 301-312.

Olasky, Susan. "Femme Fatale." *World Magazine*. 29 March 1997: 2.

Spender, Dale. *Man Made Language*. Boston: Routledge, 1981.

Spender, Dale. "Women and Literary History." *The Feminist Reader*. Eds. Catherine Belsey and Jane Moore. Malden, Mass: Blackwell Publishers, 1997: 16-25.

St. Joseph Foundation and Friends. "Inclusive Language: A Violation of Our Rights." 27 July 2006 <www.ewtn.com/library>.

Tannen, Deborah. *Talking from 9-5*. New York: William Morrow and Company, 1994.

Tobias, Sheila. *Faces of Feminism*. Boulder, Colorado: Westview Press, 1997.

Tompkins, Jane. *Sensational Designs*. New York: Oxford University Press.

Wolf, Naomi. *The Beauty Myth*. New York: Perennial, 2002.

Wood, Julia T. *Gendered Lives: Communication, Gender, and Culture*. New York: Wadsworth, 2001.

Woolf, Virginia. "Professions for Women." *One Hundred Great Essays*. Ed. Robert DiYanni. New York: Longman, 2002: 774-779.

CHAPTER IV

HOW WE READ AND INTERPRET LITERATURE

On a deconstruction model of textuality, literary texts do not hold still and docilely submit themselves to repeated identical readings; they can be read and reread, and each reading differs from the last.
  —Sharon Crowley (20)

The circumstances within which a reader encounters a literary text are always, in this broad sense, political, since they always involve preferences, interests, tastes, and beliefs that are not universal but part of the particular reader's situation.
  —Jane Tompkins (9)

Professor Andrew Bailey gazed up from his *Portable Hawthorne* to see that it was well past midnight. Outside the wind blew coldly, creating little tempests and threatening whirlwinds across his window. At times, thought the professor, the snow seemed to conspire with the wind to form hoary little ghosts that danced erratically across his home--screaming moans of displeasure. Inside, the focus was on one of Bailey's favorite literary characters—Hester Prynne. On a night like this, with only the torrents of snow to keep him company, Bailey could admire Prynne even more. She was, he thought, an intrepid woman who faced the climate, the social oppression, and salient misogyny of her time with unparalleled courage and grace. The wind outside continued to drift as Bailey's thoughts wandered to the recent death of his mother. Hester had become even more significant since his mother's tragic fall to cancer. The death had caused Bailey to reconsider all of the female protagonists in his literature. Few garnered more praise than the independent-minded Hester—the woman who had the tenacity to raise a child alone, to remain steadfast and resolved despite her disaffected status among the Puritans with whom she lived.

Again Bailey's thoughts turned to his mother and the fortitude she had shown through his years as an undergraduate and then through graduate school. Until Bailey was awarded a teaching assistantship, it had been his mother who had supplied the needed funds as well as moral support. Never, thought Bailey, did she ever think of herself during those trying times after the loss of her husband. Like Hester, his mother had been a mother and father when he needed both most.

It was now well past one o'clock and the endless, ubiquitous deluge of flakes continued to cascade from the sky. Still, Bailey had a lecture to prepare and his reminiscing had provided fodder for an inspired look at Hester and her thematic significance. As Bailey began to compose, he remembered lectures he had given in previous years on Hester and *The Scarlet Letter*. They had often been scathing attacks on her passivity, her silly willingness to shield Dimmesdale and allow him to live a fraudulent life with impunity. Now, however, with the memory of his mother being such a stark and dramatic memory, he would prepare a response that reflected his altered vision. Hester, at least for the time being, had regained her lofty place in his pantheon of literary heroes....

Shelley Lang

Shelley stepped away from the computer and tried to compose herself. She had an essay to write on *The Scarlet Letter* but was uncertain as to how to articulate her emotions. As a devout Christian, she felt genuine anger at the novel and the way Hester's illegitimate child was being romanticized by the author and the entire class she was in. Hester had engaged in adultery with a minister and lived among the other Puritans with her illegitimate child, working among the community and gradually finding forgiveness and even admiration for her modest demeanor and hard work. As a person who opposed the immorality of premarital sex and who felt contempt for adultery, Shelley wanted to write an essay that clearly and forcefully voiced her disdain for the story and the suggestion that Hester was actually the most honest and genuine person in the town. Certainly we all have our secrets, but Hester's characterization in the novel seemed to legitimize her actions and make them seem acceptable.

Finally, she returned to her computer and began crafting her rough draft. Despite her professor's admiration for Hester and the novel, she would write a scathing attack on the lack of realism and the weaknesses of Romantic writers like Hawthorne. She knew that such behavior was not acceptable then and caused myriad social problems in her own time. In the novel's end, Dimmesdale dies but Hester lives on with her illegitimate child. Shelley would write that such Romantic motifs made Hester's actions seem acceptable and demonized the religious community. It was typical of the skewed values of Romantic writers like Thoreau, Hawthorne, and Emerson, and Shelly was not timid about exposing this to the class.

Andre Carter

It had been five years since the city riots, but Andre Carter, an African American, was again contemplating their relevance. Part of the reason for Andre's interest in the riots was his reading of Jean Rousseau's *Social Contract*. For Carter, Rousseau's eighteenth-century treatise was the quintessential justification for the kind of disobedience that had transpired during those violent evenings after the "not guilty" verdict of two White police officers. The pages turned, and Andre smiled. Rousseau seemed to anticipate the oppression of African Americans in his essay, in his references to the slave who was placed in fetters against his will, in his vehement vilification of slavery as being "against nature." Also, important, thought Andre, was the responsibility that the government had toward its people—the duty it had to protect and assure a context of liberty and equality. "There will always be a vast difference," argued Rousseau, "between subduing a mob and governing a social group" (64). When people, or a group of people, failed to be served by the government—when the social contract was violated--there was no logical solution but to resort to violence, to reclaim one's part of the historical pact.

Andre's thoughts again returned to the riots and the looting that had occurred. As a Black man, he was proud of his people and their unwillingness to be subjugated and ignored. Rousseau's literature had helped fortify his beliefs in the necessity of violent responses to social injustice. Wasn't it Rousseau who had said, "man is born free and everywhere he is in chains"? Tomorrow he would return to class and again argue in support of the riots and the real meaning of Rousseau's words. Perhaps he would invoke the words of Locke and Hobbes as well. White people didn't understand because words of natural freedom meant little to people who had never been enslaved. The literature exposed real, genuine truths, and it was his intention to articulate them to his college peers. Andre understood Rousseau in a personal way and wanted to share his truths with his fellow students, to enlighten them to his vision.

Skip Letterman

Skip was in fine form as he finished the first paragraph of his response on Rousseau and his *Social Contract*. Above anything, Skip wanted his audience to understand that riots and resistance were never an alternative to measured and patient diplomacy, and he rejected the idea of violence as a vehicle for solving problems. When people took matters into their own hands, anarchy ensued, which led to more random violence and chaos. In many ways, Skip didn't like Rousseau's work, since it seemed to suggest that citizens had the right and even obligation to confront a government that seemed unresponsive to their needs and to even engage in violent resistance. This could never be. Skip considered the discussion the class had engaged in earlier in the week and wondered why some of the minority students felt so inspired by *Social Contract*. It was government that protected people from their savage inclinations, from their desire to simply steal and pillage. In short, this was not a piece of writing that responded to modern day concerns about police justice. Many of his peers were simply misreading the literature, and his personal response would clarify the matter. Injustice must be remedied with circumspection and reflection. The rule of law must always prevail in a civilized society.

Bart Miller

Bart Miller smiled as he finished his journal response to Dickens's *Great Expectations* and read over his prose. Few of his peers appreciated or even enjoyed the nineteenth-century novel, but Miller felt a fulminating sense of identification as he considered the plot and its main character Pip. Like Bart, Pip was a poor, uneducated boy who had learned to recognize the importance of friendship and loyalty. Never did Bart hate Pip more than when he shunned his brother-in-law Joe. Never did Bart feel more joy than when Pip rejoined his brother-in-law and the values he embodied. As a teenager in a lower-middle-class family, Bart had often felt the sting of being ostracized, of being different. Sometimes there wasn't enough money for social events, and Bart's clothes exposed his family's meager income. All of that alienation, however, had been replaced with pride now.

In Pip, Bart had a person whom he could admire and from whom he could gain confidence. Here was a boy who had gone from poverty to wealth and had learned the hollowness of riches without love. The parade of opulence, from Miss Havisham to Estella had all been insignificant when compared to the devotion he had received from Joe. There was something more to life than the accumulation of wealth. Money and its trappings had done little for Estella and even less for the bitter Miss Havisham. Perhaps, he thought, it was silly to invest so much in wealth when it generated happiness for so few. Perhaps, there was something more that others were missing in their new cars and designer clothes.

As he turned the page, he tried to envision Estella. As a senior who had lofty goals for college and his career, he knew he would meet many materialistic people like her--people who valued extrinsic rewards and the trumpery of an affluent life. And he knew that he would never make the mistake of becoming enamored by such people or lifestyles. Unlike Pip, he was confident in who he was and no experience at a large university would ever cause him to betray his parents, his heritage, or his culture.

As Bart closed the book and prepared for bed, he remembered the words of Willy Loman, a tragic character in *Death of a Salesman*. As with *Great Expectations*, this drama had also touched him and forced him to reconsider his values. Willy was forever trying to plant something, forever attempting to create a foundation for his life. The root cause of his problem and those of Miss Havisham and Magwitch was avarice. It was as Thoreau had said in his discussion of living a life of quiet desperation. Bart smiled and began the short trek to his bedroom. Never would he become victim to greed and superficiality. His education had come from a mother and father who worked hard and valued education and personal, philosophical happiness. It was a way of life that was fortified by the literature he read.

Chad Beckwith

Chad Beckwith had completed his essay on Dickens's *Great Expectations* and began to read over his prose and proofread for errors. Outside of his home the wind swirled the snow and rattled the trees. It was cold, and Chad wondered why literature always tried to make poor people look so positive. "If someone is poor it is because they're incompetent or lazy," he said to himself as he took a break from his essay. "And yet," he thought, "the story had tried to make the wealthy people unhappy because they were missing something important in their personal lives." His paper reflected the contention that Pip's story seemed hard to believe and was almost incredulous to him. As a young man who had grown up around money—both of his parents were doctors—he thought it was rather silly to suggest that the poor could make it by simply doing a good deed for someone. Pip was not an admirable character to Chad. He didn't like Pip's clumsiness, his poor background, or the notion that people make it in life by being given secret allotments of money. His paper was a forceful condemnation of the novel and the world that Dickens tried to create through his characters and plots. It seemed that the wealthy were always villains to Dickens, and Chad wondered why. They were always Ebeneezer Scrooge or someone similar in cruelty. Such characterizations were not fair and not realistic.

Chad finished his essay and smiled. This was one of the best papers he had ever crafted. It was an eloquent defense of wealth and even greed. People were rich because they worked for it. Dickens's world simply didn't make sense and tended to propagate a simplistic world perspective about wealth and money. For some reason, writers liked to vilify those with money, but the truth was much different, and this was the theme of Chad's masterpiece.

The Myth Of Objective Interpretations

When we read literature, we engage in a very personal literary transaction—a sharing of our values and perceptions with those of the author. While many of us have been told that there is a single or correct interpretation to the stories we read, the truth is much more dynamic and organic. Each time we pick up a poem or story, we bring our model of the world to the event and imbue that piece of literature with our model. The way we perceive characters and our interpretation of their actions, are shaped by our background, culture, and values. The respected literary critic Louise Rosenblatt compares reading a story to a creative event—something that happens in a dynamic and intimate encounter. Whether we are Black or White—male or female—we are affected by our past and hopes for the future when we read a piece of writing. This is why leading experts in the teaching of reading literature see it as a creative action. When we read a book, we are actively involved in building and constructing a story rather than passively processing words. This is how literature is read or created by a reader. As Rosenblatt said in her book *The Reader, the Text, the Poem*, "the poem must be thought of as an event in time. It is not an object or an ideal entity. It happens during a coming together, a compenetration of a reader and a text. The reader brings to the text his past experience and present personality" (12).

For years, students of literature have labored under the illusion that the novels, poems, and short stories they read are forever fixed in time and impervious to personal interpretation. Indeed, much of this sentiment was fortified by a series of prescriptive books that presented literature study as an objective regimen that was governed by impersonal interpretation. The New Critics, explains Charles Bressler, developed a theory which perceived literature as "possessing its own being and existing...like any other object. In effect, a poem becomes an artifact, an objective, self-contained autonomous entity with its own structure" (35).

Of course, as the examples I began the chapter with demonstrate, literature is rarely fixed in time or autonomous. Rather than being like a museum relic, from which others garner information, a piece of literature is more analogous to a relationship that is ongoing and fluid. Each time we pick up a novel, poem, or book and become immersed in its words and collaborate in creating its meaning—one that might never exist again and one that mirrors the nuances of the time in which we read—we are crafting a new and very individual reading of the story. As we read and interact with the images on the page, we contribute to those images, shaping them to fit our model of the world and our many emotions toward it. And as with any conversation, our reading is affected by the drama of the moment—by the pressures of the time, by the perspective we have about the people we read, by the mood in which we read. "Literature is nothing," adds Robert Probst "until a reader picks up the page, reads and responds to it, and therefore transforms it into an event" (7). It is, to be sure, an event that is created by both an author and a reader—joined by a moment in time.

Thus, it seems imperative that any discussion of reading and interpretation address literature and its fluid, mercurial character. When we approach a novel, poem, or short story as if it contains a single truth that only needs to be unearthed by an experienced reader, we pervert the very essence of the literary experience. We make it a bloodless scholastic exercise rather than a personal journey. Removed from the activity is the democratic component that allows all of us to enjoy literature in our own fashion. Again, Robert Probst speaks elegantly to this subject when he asserts that literature "is not the private domain of an intellectual elite. It is instead the reservoir of all mankind's concerns" (7).

Democracy and Reading

Many experts who study literary criticism wonder if people can have a truly meaningful reading experience if they are not permitted to read literature in their own way and contribute their own interpretation to the text. We rarely think of politics when discussing literature and language, but if we are not allowed to infuse the literary experience with our values and if we are not allowed to process it through our own prism, we forfeit the democratic sharing of ideas that should be inherent in a literary activity. Thus, many who teach English discuss the importance of evoking literature from a "Reader Response Approach." To do this is not to say that any random interpretation is valid. The Reader Response theory requires a close scrutiny of what is written and an accurate depiction of the story or essay being discussed. However, it also invites readers to incorporate their feelings as they react to the words on the page.

Andre's reading of Rousseau was clearly different than Skip Letterman's, despite the fact that they read the same words. What makes literature exciting and relevant is the fact that they can use it as a catalyst for their modern-day discussions and differences. It is the springboard from which democratic debates soar and ideals about government and freedom can be considered. To say that one reading is better than another would be to alienate one of the readers and remove the most important aspect of reading from its process—inclusive expression. "The only way to exclude readers from making meaning is to assume that a text has one correct interpretation, that it is univocal—speaks with one voice" (63) argues Cleo Cherryholmes. And yet, the idea of transaction suggests that reading is never a monologue but a broad discussion of various voices. Authors share their vision of the world through their writing and rewriting of the novel, while readers transact with these images and apply their own paradigm to the experience—one that often changes as they read and interact in the world.

Something To Think About

Think about your reading of a book or poem and consider the various reactions you had to characters and scenes. How much of your reading was affected by your own vision of the world and your system of values? Now contrast your interpretation of a book or movie—or any text—from someone else who experienced the same event. How was each of your "readings" colored by your background? The recent movie *Brokeback Mountain* (2006) is about two modern day cowboys who struggle to understand their homosexual feelings, their ill-conceived marriages, and the possibility of ever being together. In watching this film, people's reactions are dramatically affected by their social values and feelings about homosexuality. It is also driven by the beautiful scenery, the attitudes the audience has toward marriage and even fidelity and love. While most critics see the film as an unmitigated success, many social critics argue about its importance as a social statement and their personal transaction with this cinematic text. What was yours? Why did you react the way you did?

Volumes of research have explored the literary experience and revealed its very active and aesthetic nature. However, beyond all of the research lies the concrete, daily examples that all who read or teach literature know about. As a reader and a teacher of English, I can see the endearing essence of literature in the very idiosyncratic responses of my students when they're truly interacting with a text. For these kids and young adults, literature is a pleasurable and even riveting exploration, a meaningful engagement with a book. It is important to appreciate the transactions most students have with fiction and the reason why such an experience is vital to the teaching of literature. Also important is a complete understanding of the theoretical foundations upon which literary instruction is predicated.

The Traditional Way To Read: The New Critics

Fifty years ago, much of the literary instruction was governed by the theories of the New Critics. As a group, these scholars tended to see the literary experience as containing a correct answer, as being an activity that needed careful guidance so that neophytes wouldn't allow their feelings to infringe upon their work and evoke erroneous interpretations. In exploring this philosophy, one must consider the work of Mortimer Adler, who defined the era by writing a work titled *How to Read a Book*. In Adler's philosophy, which prescribed neat, almost clinical steps in the correct reading of a text, we find the top-down, prescriptive and singularly didactic approach to literacy that epitomizes this movement. For Adler, the act of reading begins with teachers and is often assiduously regulated by them. Like the museum guide, who explains the relics to be observed and the correct way to understand them, Adler believed that the instructor should walk students through the literary experience, protecting them from fallacies and poor methodology. To impose one's emotional response, to become engaged in what a poem does to us as we read, was pejoratively called an "affective fallacy" and was to be dutifully eschewed. Interpretation, in the world of the New Critics, was a science, a search for the ultimate truth.

Of course, such a theory is neither inclusive nor intellectual, for it relegates interpretation to a rather mechanical, perfunctory act of excavating an implanted theme. Rather than involving the life and passions of the reader in a transaction (Rosenblatt) with the text, it reduces the reading process to a single truth, usually one that is revealed in the passive process of a lecture. Thus, to relegate reading and literature to a scientific act is to invalidate the diverse and colorful responses of minority students, who find a much different relevance in works such as *Black Boy* or *The Color Purple*. The New Criticism would trivialize the feminist reaction to Chopin's *The Awakening* and militates against the kind of artistic search for truth that radiates through every meaningful interaction with a text.

Such a response, I am convinced, is a myth and a sure way to alienate readers from the kind of provocative, personally riveting experience that literature offers. Of course, no one would disagree with the contention that literature should be studied assiduously as a carefully crafted work of art. In that belief, virtually all literary critics agree. However, when one discusses the role of the reader, the place of the novel, and the authority that each wields in designing a literary response, a wedge between the New Critics and the more recent Reader Response approach begins to emerge and become evident. It is the more contemporary belief that readers must be included in every aspect of the process, that reading must be managed by a teacher but never usurped by that teacher.

The Politics Of Literary Interpretation

To best appreciate the political dynamics upon which a literary classic is made, one needs to step back and consider some of the rather curious and edifying circumstances upon which certain classics have come to acquire their revered status. Where some scholars would have us believe that the formulation of a canon is a simple, deliberate act of acknowledging merit, or as Mathew Arnold said of celebrating "the best of what has been thought and said in the world" (Arnold 6), what we find is that canons are tainted with politics and power struggles. Far from being removed from privilege, classic works usually reflect the visions of those in authority and the values they wish to promote.

In some cases, they mirror Arnold's desire to "civilize" the masses and infuse them with the gift of culture. In such a condescending context, one sees that the recognition of great literature emanates from the upper classes, from those with power and money and the means by which to advance their agenda. The goal of such literary criticism is not egalitarian but a means of "social order" (Storey 26), as a way to create a "self perpetuating cultural elite" (272) so that the masses do not seek answers in their own voices and passions. "What it amounts to," argues John Storrey, in discussing the creation and passage of culture in such things as great books, "is essentially...the mobilization of culture to police the unruly forces of mass society" (27). "Canons arise," continues Storey, "from particular interests, located in specific social and historical contexts. They are as much about policing knowledge as they are about organizing terrains of critical inquiry" (197).

Is there an inherent greatness to the literature we study or has the interpretive process been sullied by political wrangling and power plays? In answering this question it is helpful to examine the past and the specific ways by which certain works came to be called "classics." What about Henry David Thoreau, the earthy transcendentalist, the naturalist, who represents a dual status as both an icon and iconoclast in our national pantheon. In considering a man like Thoreau——so revered and celebrated——one would expect a long and rather consistent line of praise for his work. Because he is considered a writer of great works, those that stand the test of time, those that are ostensibly beyond politics, there would seem to be no time in history when Thoreau was not venerated for the great writing he did. Because, as the saying goes, great literature is different from cheap culture in that it endures and transcends the time period in which it was written. It is, to put it simply, beyond time, elevated to a greatness that is beyond any era.

That is what makes Henry David Thoreau so fascinating. During his short but prolific life, Thoreau wrote often, but was rarely if ever exulted for the quality or eloquence of his work. Where were the critics, one wonders, when Thoreau tried to publish *Walden*, a classic that is required reading in American literature classes today? Whatever the answer, we know that Thoreau was compelled to pay for the publishing of *Walden* himself. Perry Miller, in discussing Thoreau's life, chronicles "his declining months and "the crushing reality of his failure" when musing upon his career (250). During his life, Thoreau was dwarfed by the celebrity of Longfellow, Lowell, and Bryant—poets who are curiously almost forgotten in literature classes today. "And this man," adds Miller in discussing Thoreau, "has now become a God in modern literature. Wherever English is read, or can be translated, Thoreau is one of the voices of the nineteenth century..." (250).

And so, skeptics are left to wonder. If literary analysis is truly as accurate and certain as some would have us believe, why haven't the critics themselves been a little more true to their history? Great works, according to Samuel Johnson in his "Preface to Shakespeare," should withstand the test of time, beyond "whatever allusions local customs, or temporary opinions" that might have provided for temporary fame (444-445). And yet, Thoreau, Poe, and Herman Melville all are examples of how capricious literary judgments can be. Today they are exulted literary masters, but why wasn't that eloquence recognized in their own time? If, in fact, literary analysis is beyond politics, then, why was the work of Thoreau dismissed by critics in his own time?

Even the writer Nathaniel Hawthorne, argues Jane Tompkins, might have garnered much of his early status from "external circumstances" that had little to do with his true greatness. Specifically, Tompkins suggests that old fashioned nepotism almost certainly affected the context upon which Hawthorne's "Twice Told Tales" was evaluated. Longfellow's review in the *North American Review* was probably influenced by the fact that Hawthorne had been a classmate of his in college—that both "shared a common background and a common vocation"

(Tompkins 9). Equally intriguing is the fact that the editor of the *Salem Gazette*, adds Tompkins, was indebted to Hawthorne for a number of early contributions, and this created a situation for an evaluation that was clearly compromised by pecuniary as well as personal concerns. An especially revealing fact, considering the meager resources that Thoreau had throughout his life.

We now return to the absence of literature written by women, which was first discussed in the third chapter. For years it was virtually impossible to enter a college or even high school literature class and read a classic written by a woman. Even though they crafted some of the most powerful and moving works of their time, such as *Uncle Tom's Cabin*, it was considered academically improper to promote a feminist work. Why? Is this another example of objective evaluation being compromised by a decidedly misogynistic elite?

If you will remember, this is the position of Jane Tompkins, who devotes much of her book *Sensational Designs* to an examination of literature written by women—literature that despite the power and courage it displayed, was curiously excluded from a literary pantheon. Of these, *Uncle Tom's Cabin* is one of the most puzzling examples. Why, wonders Tompkins, are critics so quick to dismiss the novel simply because it falls into the category of sentimental fiction? Didn't the work, which ignited the fires of anger in the South before the Civil War, have a dramatic effect on the nation? Did it not make an indelible mark on the American psyche? "I will argue," answers Tompkins, "that the work of the sentimental writers is complex and significant in ways other than those that characterize the established masterpieces. Still," she continues, "such works of art are snubbed by academic critics because of a long tradition of academic parochialism" (125).

Tompkins is hardly the first to suggest that literary evaluation is political and subjective. In her essay "Women and Literary History," Dale Spender muses on the inaccuracies of her university education--one that blissfully negated women while promulgating a theory that all great literature was the domain of men. "No matter where I looked around me," writes Spender, "I encountered almost exclusively the publications of men. Like Virginia Woolf in the British museum, I too found that the library catalog and shelves were filled with books predominately authored by men" (16). "It had to be," he later concludes, "because women had not written books" (17). But, as Spender later realized, this was not the case. Women did write in the incipient years of the novel, many with great acumen and elegance. And yet, where did they all go? Why, she muses, was she not taught about the legacy of women in the literary world that they helped construct? Spender suggests that the exclusion of women in the literary canon is an example of sexism, selective attention to the past, and, in some cases, actual theft of literature written by women.

> In the eighteenth century, women wrote in much the same way as men, with much the same (if not greater) success than men, and attained much the same (if not more) success than men. Yet not only has this achievement of women been edited out of literary history, but a false version has been substituted in its place. A distorted version which makes no mention of women's former greatness, but which presents the birth of the novel solely in terms of men. (21)

And how have men been able to exclude women from the fruits of their literary work? In one example, Spender points to the work of D.H. Lawrence and the notes he solicited from Jessie Burrows, from his wife Freida, from writer Mabel Dodge Luhan, and others. Lawrence, also, Spender continues, "took over women's manuscripts and rewrote them, as in the cases of Helen Corke and Mollie Skinner's" (22). Equally as compelling is the contention that a male-dominated literary world simply expunged women from the pantheon once their contemporary popularity was achieved. In the eighteenth century, for example, there were plenty of great, well-respected women writers who were acknowledged in their own era but who have since been erased from the books that chronicle great novels. Why? Was it that these women's works simply did not meet the lofty requirements of a demanding literary world? Hardly. Rather, the words of writers such as Mary Wollstonecraft, Fanny Burney, Mary Hays, and Amelia Opie—an esteemed elite in the eighteenth century—were methodically expunged by male critics of the nineteenth century.

"How do we explain this transition from prominence to negation?" (20) asks Spender. While there are a series of interesting theories, the most plausible is simply that the decision making powers were concentrated in the hands of men who not surprisingly found the good and great among their fellow men" (20) Or, to put it harshly, a male-dominated society "presumes a male-dominated literary tradition as a result" (21). Power—not literary scrutiny—is the clear answer.

Real Life Transactions With A Text

Perhaps the best way to appreciate the myth of the objective approach to literature is actually to experience the reading and interacting that transpires when one reads and constructs a text. This can happen through formal classes, through personal reading, and through book clubs. In such informal settings, where readers feel liberated to speak candidly about their reactions to characters and scenes, one can begin to appreciate the way stories are created through personal interactions and experience—through diving into the dilemmas, the questions, the moral ambiguities. Like a sport, reading can be done at different levels and with varying objectives. And like any artistic endeavor, it is lived and interpreted in different, equally valid ways, depending upon factors that involve reader, setting, time, and mood.

As an example, let us consider the classic *The Adventures of Huckleberry Finn*, a favorite canonical work--one that is read and debated in high schools and universities all across our country. For some African Americans, no book inspires more anger, resentment, or consternation. For me, in contrast, it is a fresh, honest, and, sometimes, dark portrait of the American spirit. In Huck Finn's whimsical, introspective character, I find a quintessential American, an allegory for the doubts and hopes of a burgeoning nation.

Of course, there are plenty of other responses and reflections. While many of my colleagues enjoy and even love the novel, they do for very different reasons—reasons that reflect their personal reading and socio-cultural background. Literature, I would like to argue, has always been a very organic, individual act. Despite the pretensions of some who believe that a book is autonomous, it is extremely difficult to find two readings of *The Adventures of Huckleberry Finn* or any work that yield uniform reactions.

A Class Responds To *The Adventures of Huckleberry Finn*

As an example, I asked an advanced class of high school seniors to examine two scenes in the novel and explain how they helped contribute to the novel's themes and character development. It was my theory that such a review would generate a plethora of unique and curious ideas—each in its own way in consonance with the personal reading of the specific person. Louise Rosenblatt, one of the most prominent scholars for the Reader Response theory that I am advocating, refers to it as an aesthetic transaction, as readers apply their model of the world, their intellectual perspective, their political views, and mood for the moment to the dynamic richness of a literary classic.

As I participated in the final exercise, reading the episodes involving the feud and the final farewell scene between Jim and Huck, I also wrote informal notes and responses. Because I had asked my students to do the same, I was hoping that the readings would generate a cavalcade of intriguing reflections and insights. Especially interesting for me was the chance to review essays I had previously written on the novel, to see how even my interpretation had been transformed through the years of maturity and shifting attitudes.

Days passed, and our class met for our forum on *Huck Finn*. From the opening words, it was clear that the novel in general and the scenes in particular had fostered a wealth of visions and perspectives. From one African-American female came questions about the portrayal of Black people in the novel. For her, the final scene redeemed Jim as an independent agent who could think for himself and live without Huck. Although much of the novel presented slaves in a dubious fashion, she considered Jim's separation from Huck, his desire to journey forward into a precarious land, as a symbol of his fortitude, character, and growth.

As expected in a democratic classroom, her reading was only the first of a beautiful literary fountain. Gary, an older White student, argued that Jim's final departure made him seem less transcendental or Romantic. Gary, who was intrigued with the works of Thoreau and Emerson, read much of the novel from a transcendental perspective. For him, Jim's final farewell was a disappointing end to a romantic odyssey, one where men of different colors and backgrounds unite with nature to uncover lofty philosophical truths.

Sandy was next to contribute. Unlike her peers, she was a self-described "Southerner" who was extremely upset with the portraits of Southern men and women in the book. In particular, Sandy's focus was on the hypocrisy of Aunt Sally and Uncle Silas, the slave-owning Christians who wanted to adopt and civilize Huck. Like Miss Watson and the Widow Douglass, the two represented a sorry contingent of cowards, rascals, racists, and con-artists—all Southerners. Sandy's objections about the portrayal was the catalyst for other discussions about history's view of the antebellum South and the "revisions" that have exacerbated any objective or plausible theory about its stature.

From this came references to William Taylor's *Cavalier and Yankee* and the premise that the Southerner was, in fact, a proud, stately gentleman farmer, in the spirit of Thomas Jefferson. Sandy was visibly upset with the caricatures that were drawn by authors and the tendency of history to be written by the victors of war rather than by truth-seeking scholars. Others, of course, saw her interpretations of the South as being indicative of a regional bias. In the end, we all agreed that literature and history are vulnerable to the currents of politics and the visceral. An African American could never identify with a White Southerner and a Yankee could never appreciate the plight of the slave. And yet, each of these responses was clearly supported by the novel. Sandy, in lamenting the castigation of the South, clearly had a legitimate point. At the same time, however, so did the majority of readers who saw the book as fair toward Southerners of the nineteenth century.

Such discussions represent only a small sampling of the literary buffet that was presented and feasted over that day. To say that literature lives in all of us—and that we live in it—is to savor the symbiotic relationship that every student shares with a text. Rather than providing us with fixed answers and monolithic truths, the great works unleash the passions and ideologies of its public, producing a tapestry of interpretations and answers. To say that literature should eschew the emotional, the idiosyncratic, is to divest it of its essence, of the blood that resonates through its pages.

How dynamic is the transaction between reader and text? How intimate and lofty are the connections? Consider Janice Radway's *Reading the Romance* and the rather curious and fascinating place that romance novels had for the population of Smithton women that Radway studied. Indeed, Radway—after extensive interviews and surveys—found that romance novels served the women to make sense of their own lives while offering them a cathartic escape from the patriarchy in which they lived. Perhaps, what was most revealing about the work was the active way the women manipulated the books, based on the social and cultural verities in their lives. Only certain romances were accepted because only particular plots and characters fit congruently and comfortably into their model of the world. Indeed, it is entirely possible to believe that a group of more educated women would have responded quite differently to the romance.

In the end, then, we are left with a vision of a novel or poem that is much more analogous to a beautiful portrait than a recipe for a cake. The myth that one reads great poetry with a bloodless, sterile, scientific approach is simply erroneous as well as despotic and arrogant. Skepticism has always been a part of the human psyche. To close off that spirit of experimentation, that healthy, explorative trait, is to strip reading of its essence, of its ability to speak to different people in contrasting ways, depending upon the context and the transaction between reader and author.

Works Cited

Adler, Mortimer. *How to Read a Book*. New York: Simon and Schuster, 1940.

Arnold, Mathew. *Culture and Anarchy*. London: Cambridge University Press, 1960.

Bressler, Charles. *Literary Criticism: An Introduction to Theory and Practice*. Englewood Cliffs, New Jersey: Prentice Hall, 1994.

Cherryholmes, Cleo. *Power and Criticism*. New York: Teachers College Press, 1988.

Chopin, Kate. *The Awakening*. New York: Penguin Books, 1984.

Crowley, Sharon. *A Teacher's Introduction to Deconstruction*. Urbana, IL: National Council of Teachers of English, 1989.

Dickens, Charles. *Great Expectations*. New York: Globe, 1986.

Johnson, Samuel. "Preface to Shakespeare." *The Great Critic*s. Eds. James Harry Smith and Edd Winfield Parks, New York: W.W. Norton and Company, 1951. 444-445.

Miller, Arthur. *The Death of a Salesman*. New York: Penguin, 1949.

Miller, Perry. "Walden—The Secret Center." *Walden*. New York: Signet Books, 1960.

Probst, Robert. *Response and Analysis*. Portsmouth, NH: Heinemann, 1988.

Radway, Janice. *Reading the Romance*. Chapel Hill: University of North Carolina Press, 1984.

Rosenblatt, Louise. *The Reader, The Text, The Poem*. Carbondale: Southern Illinois University Press, 1978.

Rousseau, Jean. "The Origin of Civil Society." *A World of Ideas*. Boston: St. Martin's Press, 1990. 56-73.

Spender, Dale. "Women and Literary History." *The Feminist Reader*. Malden, MA: Blackwell, 1989.

Storey, John. *An Introduction to Cultural Theory and Popular Culture*. Athens: University of Georgia Press, 1998.

Taylor, William. *Cavalier and Yankee*. New York: George Braziller, 1961.

Tompkins, Jane. *Sensational Designs*. New York: Oxford University Press, 1985.

Twain, Mark. *The Adventures of Huckleberry Finn*. New York: Bantam, 1965.

CHAPTER V

LEARNING AND DEVELOPING LANGUAGE

The limits of my language mean the limits of my world.
—Ludwig Wittgenstein

To watch an infant learn language is truly an impressive and mysterious phenomenon. Without a day of formal education and devoid of even a single grammar book, the child masters the language of his/her speech community, developing from one linguistic stage to the next. And this is not an event that occurs for only the exceptionally bright child. With interaction and reasonable intelligence, every child of every culture of the world learns how to speak. It is as natural and predictable as walking. How amazing is the acquisition of language? Linguist Arlene Moskowitz explains it this way:

> The speed with which children accomplish the complex
> process of language acquisition is particularly impressive.

Ten linguists working full time for ten years to analyze the structure of the English language could not program a computer with the ability for language acquired by an average child in the first ten years or even five years of life. (86)

This chapter is about language acquisition and development, because as we learn more about the process of language growth, we also learn important facts about ourselves as language users and students. Most students of English come to class with the notion that they need to study their language and learn grammar. Years of schooling have taught them to feel insecure about their linguistic acumen and inherent skill. The fact is, we learn language in a very natural and social way and this is true of all language endeavors, whether it is speaking, reading, or writing. It is not something that is taught but something that is nurtured, guided, and occasionally coached. As we realize that all language skills are connected, we come to understand the parallels between learning speech and learning to read and write. In each endeavor, it is a natural extension of our social lives, a natural absorption of the information in our world, and should be treated that way. Whether one is learning to speak, read, or write, the motivation is essentially the same. Children—or adults—are trying to make sense of their world through the use of language.

Equally important is the fact that language is something we construct as we listen to the people around us and formulate theories as to how language works. It is not something that we receive passively but something we build and rebuild throughout our lives. If we are lucky, we devote our entire existence to improvement and refinement of our language. This is something that begins with childhood and is typified by an indefatigable search for meaning. Again, linguist Arlene Moskowitz is helpful when she suggests that "the picture that is emerging from the more sophisticated investigations reveals the child as an active language learner, continually analyzing what she hears and proceeding in a methodical way to put together the jigsaw puzzle of language" (88).

The Need For Social Interaction

All of us learn language in stages or episodes, leading experts to see language development as a process. Without the time and nurturing that are part of this process, one will not learn to become literate. A second ingredient that is critical to the acquisition of language is social interaction. If we are not given ample opportunity to interact with language users and practice our linguistic skills with those who possess a more advanced language ability, we will not develop as speakers, readers, or writers. Scientists agree that there is a "critical period" in the learning of language and argue that people who are not allowed socialization and interaction with language during this critical period will never learn language normally.

Perhaps, the most celebrated researcher on the theory of a critical period in language growth is Eric Lenneberg, who was one of the first to suggest that people have a certain period in their lives when their brains are more open and elastic to language growth. In this critical period, Lenneberg posited that the brain's two hemispheres were more malleable to language reception, that they could be used in concert to develop the child's complete language development. After the critical period, he suggested that "lateralization" (localization to one hemisphere of the brain) occurred, which precluded language acquisition. "After puberty," writes Lenneberg, "the ability for self organization and adjustment to the physiological demands of verbal behavior quickly declines. The brain behaves as if it has become set in its ways and primary, basic skills not acquired by that time usually remain deficient for life" (158).

Indeed, studies of the brain and language have shown that both the right and left hemispheres contribute to language activity during the critical period in a child's language growth. However, this phenomenon must be stimulated by the language and nurture of others. While brain imaging shows that the left hemisphere deals primarily with language, it seems clear that the right is instrumental in the development of metaphorical language and more large-scale aspects of communication. Early in life, these hemispheres work in concert as the child tests and retests hypothesis to acquire language. "Thus," writes linguist Gabrielle Rico Lusser, "we begin to see that any language use of comparative richness and complexity demands active right-brain involvement. In natural writing," she adds, "each hemisphere plays an intense-ly cooperating role" (81).

But what also seems clear is that the capacity to become language users is contingent upon children's ability to hear it in their environment and use in a risk-free, experimental, heuristic way. As we grow older, our brains tend to specialize, using certain hemispheres of the brain—mostly the left—for language use. If we do not learn language during the critical period of our lives, our brains tend to respond to language in a more mechanical, less fluid way. Language stops being a natural endeavor, as any adult who has tried to learn a foreign language can attest to. Rather than being a seamless part of one's growth, it is marked with awkward pronunciations and mechanically clumsy sentences. While we often learn words in isolation—a left hemisphere function—we grapple to learn the imagery and figurative aspects of language in its holistic entirety, which is part of the right hemisphere.

One scenario that experts use in illustrating language's social character is Genie, a young girl who lived the first fourteen years of her life in virtual isolation, away from language and deprived of society of any kind. Genie's case is truly unique in its bizarre and cruel aspects. As a child, Genie was removed from family and placed on a seat that served as her chair and toilet. Here, she was fed and left alone. Her father was mentally deranged and forced Genie's disabled mother to keep their daughter in these inhumane conditions until authorities discovered the situation fourteen years after her birth. By this time, Genie had developed limited language skills and conducted herself with virtually no verbalization. Gradually, with intensive work from language experts, Genie began to utter words and short phrases but never learned to construct the complex, grammatically coherent sentences that one expects of any five-year-old language user. In short, Genie had missed the "critical period" in language development and was relegated to a linguistic life that would never see her use language in the swift, flowing way that one expects during any social conversation.

What happened to Genie? Experts believe that language acquisition is natural but not automatic. Linguist Noam Chomsky has argued that humans are unique in their ability to acquire language and has suggested that there is a learning device inside of our minds that is analogous to a light switch, responding to verbal exchanges in our environment and developing with rich linguistic support. However, it seems clear that this "linguistic light" must have the stimulation of language for it to be generated. Without the natural currents of language running through our world, we will not learn language. It is, in effect, generated and later cultivated by speakers in our surroundings. And so, when parents wonder if language development is about nurture or nature, we must answer by saying both. The first chapter of *How Babies Talk* concludes with the following statement:

> Nature has exquisitely prepared infants (and even fetuses) with the tools for analyzing the language they hear around them. Yet it is through nurture—or the environment that we provide—that babies are able to bring these innate abilities to bear. (Golinkoff & Hirsh-Pasek 10-11)

This is true of all language endeavors and offers us valuable lessons about the way we learn and grow as readers, writers, and speakers. We learn language most effectively when we are provided with a safe and rich linguistic setting—when we are immersed in language and invited to learn it at our own speed and in our direction. This is the typical way that most infants acquire language, which is why the process seems so invisible and effortless. Most parents are incredibly good language teachers because they teach very little, while creating a fun and fulfilling context for growth. As with most learning endeavors, speech does not have to be taught, but must be cultivated by people who care about the language user and respect the method by which he or she chooses to acquire the skill. "People help infants to become experts," writes author Frank Smith. "There is no formal instruction, no special time when they are expected to learn. Instead," adds Smith, "someone helps them to say what they are trying to say and to understand. The help is always relevant, so that the learner never has to ask or wonder what it is for" (3). Or, as researcher Nigel Hall adds, "What is a necessary condition of language learning is the existence of a context where children can grow surrounded by purposeful and meaningful uses of language" (13).

Meet Samantha and Linda

A good example is Samantha, who has a two-year-old daughter, Linda, at home with her. While Samantha talks to her daughter each day, she rarely corrects her speech and encourages every word and garbled phrase that is uttered from her daughter's growing lexicon. Linda's world is one of total acceptance, one that is devoid of tests, coercion, or required objectives. Instead, Linda samples from the myriad sentences in her home and gradually acquires a model of the grammar being used, making mistakes often as she experiments with the rudiments of the language.

For the first five years of her life, Linda will not be subjected to any type of language instruction but will complete her first five years with a language skill that transcends anything that could be taught by even the most advanced linguist. For instance, Linda will know that the verb precedes the noun when asking a question and know inherently that the sentence "Father Jones can be a card when asked to play" is much different semantically than "Father Jones plays cards well when asked." She will be able to know that "The freening garzal loosted the gup" is grammatically viable but semantically incoherent. She will understand that "cover your bare butt" is quite different from "Teddy Bear is a warm cover in bed but not as good as a blanket."

In short, Linda will learn the language's many components and parts. She will create sentences that are semantic (meaningful) syntactic (structurally correct) and lexical, (using the right word in the right context) and do so without even a single day in Linguistics 101. Clearly, language is a natural part of our lives when the social interaction is cultivated in an inclusive context. Equally evident is the fact that children learn language actively rather than being passively taught it by a parent. Again, Hall is helpful when he reminds us that "children play the major role in constructing their knowledge of oral language. Parents and caregivers greatly facilitate but seldom instruct children in oral language" (15).

But what do we mean when we say language is social and natural? First, it means that language is learned most effectively by simply being placed in situations where it is used, where models of it can be studied by young, aspiring speakers. Linda grows as a speaker with the help of her mother and family members and this help is devoid of any risk or punishment. Learning is done best when it is practiced with impunity and this is especially true for language. As Linda observes her world, she notices the print on cereal boxes and realizes that the McDonald's sign is a symbol for food and fun. When her Uncle Greg comes to see her, she is greeted with laughter and love after pronouncing his name "Geg." And as Linda listens to her mom talk to her Uncle Greg, she understands the way language is used by listening and experimenting. It is understood that kids need time and space to learn language and they do so in their own way. This is why almost everyone learns speech. It is the one language skill that is fostered by encouragement and nurtured with acceptance.

Perhaps, the best example for the social aspect of language development comes from author and educator Frank Smith. In his book *Joining the Literacy Club*, Smith argues that learning any language skill—whether it is reading, writing, or speech—is simply an endeavor in being accepted into one's language community or "club." Smith further suggests that joining a speech "club" is integral to a child's growth as a human and is done with significant commitment to personal identity. "Our own particular language is an emblem of all our cultural ties. Language is as personal and as significant as clothing, hairstyle, and ornamentation," writes Smith (4).

As the children listen to their mother, father, and siblings speak, they yearn to join them and become part of this social endeavor—this club. What makes speech so successful is the club-like atmosphere, where one is accepted as a member, as a special person who enjoys all of the advantages of being part of this community. They share speech with others and flourish in the sense of solidarity. "Infants are admitted as junior members. Mistakes are expected, not frowned upon or punished as undesirable behavior." In short, concludes Smith, "People help infants become experts" and they are "quickly admitted into a full range of club activities" (3). It is not surprising that the club metaphor works so well in depicting the way literacy is learned.

Meet Carlos

Carlos is a Cuban-American, born in Bronx, New York, raised in

Miami, Florida, and now residing in Flint, Michigan. Carlos is a good example of how children effortlessly absorb the languages in their environment and how social this process actually is. As a child, he heard nothing but Spanish from his parents and learned their Cuban Spanish within a few years after being born. As he continued to grow and began to socialize with his neighbors and their kids, he quickly acquired English, becoming an enthusiastic part of this new and exciting language community. Later, after his mother was given a generous promotion at work, the family hired an Italian nanny to care for Carlos and teach him the Italian language. Quickly, Carlos forged a special friendship with Maria the nanny and was learning Italian as fluidly as he learned Spanish and English.

By the time Carlos reached junior high school, he was fluent in three languages and spoke each without any of the stiff accents or foreign intonations that are heard from second language learners. At an early age—during our critical period—we learn languages in much the same fluid way that we learn to walk or tie our shoes. It becomes a rite of passage and an essential part of who we are. During the critical period in our linguistic development, our minds are absorbent sponges to the languages in our environment and language acquisition becomes a ubiquitous and invisible event.

What can we glean from Carlos? First, we should recognize the fact that he learned all three languages—as all kids learn language—without any technical help. His parents, friends, and nanny had no linguistic expertise and spent no time reviewing parts of speech with Carlos. Acquiring a language is not about being taught but being given the opportunity to learn and Carlos quickly became trilingual through a process that was fostered and actively learned. Early in Carlos's childhood he declared to a friend, "I don't want any candy." Later, when he entered his home and spoke to his family in Spanish, he professed to his mother that he didn't want nothing ("No quiero nada").

Who told Carlos that double negatives are expected in Spanish but are nonstandard in English? The next day, Carlos told his mother that he would clean the bathroom, which is pronounced banjo. All Spanish nouns have gender, so when Carlos threw his rags in the garbage, he correctly referred to it as the basura. In Spanish, bathrooms are masculine and end in the vowel "o," while the garbage is feminine and ends in the vowel "a." Again nobody told or taught Carlos the rules about gendered nouns, but he knew them and was equally successful when he told his teacher at his English speaking school that he was going to use the "bathroom."

Carlos, like all children who learn language, can use the masculine nouns of Spanish and the gender-free nouns in English. Without ever being exposed to linguistics, he is able to become a sophisticated language user, navigating his way through the nuances of each language. Carlos may never take a class in the structure of the languages he speaks, but that will have no influence on his ability to speak them astutely.

In observing the language acquisition of young children linguist Constance Weaver concludes by offering the following points:

> The grammatical system children learn is complex and abstract; it can be captured in sometimes elegant rules, but these are not rules that adults typically know or could teach. Children develop increasingly sophisticated hypotheses about the structure of their language—hypotheses that can be expressed in the form of rules that explain their grammatical competence and are responsible for their actual language performance. (38)

Chomsky and Skinner

What we learn from these examples can perhaps best be understood by looking at the celebrated disagreement between linguist Noam Chomsky and behavioral psychologist B.F. Skinner. Both are internationally venerated for their work in learning and language. Yet, when it came to the development of speech, they propagated antithetical theories for how children learn to speak. For Skinner, language development was simply a matter of reinforcement and what he termed "operant conditioning." Skinner believed that children learn language in much the same way that animals learn to perform rudimentary skills such as pecking at a certain button to get food. Rewards or positive reinforcement triggered certain behavior while negative behavior was thwarted with negative reinforcement or punishment. Like other behavioral psychologists, he embraced the notion that language was taught and that the speaker who learned language was essentially passive, learning what was encouraged and failing to learn that which was not. The following quotation from Skinner's *Verbal Behavior* captures the essence of his behavioristic approach:

> In all verbal behavior under stimulus control there
> are three important events to be taken into account: a
> stimulus, a response and a reinforcement. These are
> contingent upon each other. (81)

Chomsky disagreed, arguing that children learned language rather than it being taught. Chomsky rightly observed that children are creative when generating language and constructing sentences and words they have never heard before. What is especially revealing about children is the way they make mistakes and what those mistakes tell us about their language development. Young Carlos, for example, often would tell his teachers that he "brung" the ball in from recess, when the correct verb form is, of course, "brought." Here, Carlos was demonstrating his theory of verb formation by hypothesizing that the past tense of the verb "bring" is "brung," just as the past tense of the verb "ran" is "run." In essence, Carlos has formulated general theories about language that reveal his active attempt to make language rather than simply repeating what he hears. He is being creative, even in the mistakes he makes. Certainly, he never heard an adult use the word "brung" in a sentence but has assumed that it is the logical way to make it past tense.

Thus, Chomsky argued that children learn to talk by formulating their own theories about language from an innate ability to acquire and develop speech. It is something that is with them at birth and that grows when it is stimulated by discourse in society. "Language seems to me to grow in the mind rather as familiar physical systems of the body grow" wrote Chomsky in describing speech. "This series of changes seems to me analogous to the growth of organs" (Chomsky 139). In fact, as Heny reminds us, "Chomsky claims, humans could never learn systems as complex as natural language by simply hearing sentences" (170).

Perhaps, the best way to explain the rift between Skinner and Chomsky is to use an example. Sammy is a young boy learning English in his home. As Sammy listens to his parents and older siblings, he gradually acquires a model of English, its rules of word formation and sentence construction. What is interesting about Sammy—and what seems to validate Chomsky's creative approach to language—is that he often utters novel expressions that have nothing to do with what he has heard in his language community. One day, Sammy told his mom, "I eated the candy."

"You ate the candy," his mother said in trying to help her infant son. Again, Sammy repeated the sentence in the way he understood it at the time. "I eated it."

Despite repeated attempts to teach Sammy the correct way to compose the sentence, Sammy's mother was essentially unsuccessful. Why? Because children learn language in stages that have to do with their gradual understanding of speech. While they use their environment to learn language, it is something they do themselves and in their own time. Later, Sammy commented that his mommy had "buyed" many nice things at the store. Again, Sammy was trying to form the past tense of the verb by using his personally constructed theory of how verbs are formed. This is not something he was taught or heard but a rule he produced as he made sense of the language.

The distinction between Skinner and Chomsky can best be described as Nativism vs. Empiricism. The Nativist believes that language is inherent or innate—that it is part of the person's biological make up. This is Chomsky's view and is supported by the incredible capacity of all children to learn language without instruction and to produce unique sentences and words that reflect their evolving understanding of speech. Of course, Chomsky concedes that language is contingent upon linguistic stimulation, which is where Skinner enters the picture. Skinner argued that children are taught language and respond specifically to what they are instructed or encouraged to do. Thus, experience—or empiricism—plays an integral role in the child's language development. Of course, our earlier example of Genie is instructive. Because this traumatized child was never exposed to language and never given any linguistic stimulation, she never matured as a language user. Clearly, environment and experience are important, but these factors work only to assist the child in their active drive to learn the language by testing and revising their theories about speech patterns and word use. Constance Weaver makes an elegant observation when she argues, "what the child brings to the language-learning task, then, includes an innate ability to generate, test, and develop increasingly sophisticated hypotheses about the nature of the world in general and language in particular" (Weaver 80).

Something To Think About

If you have the opportunity, listen to a five-year-old use language and notice the way it is constructed, the words used, and the expressions formed. Is there evidence of a Nativist or Empiricist point of view? Do you hear your child produce sentences or words that are novel, suggesting a creative language capacity? How much does positive reinforcement influence the child in learning language? Can language be taught or is it a result of the child's personal understanding of what he/she hears and understands? How can we explain the fact that all children experience the same stages of language development? And finally, if children are taught language, how do we explain their understanding of complicated aspects of speech that they were never taught?

Transcription vs. Transaction

Connie Weaver, whom I quoted earlier, has suggested that language development can best be explained by distinguishing between transcription and transaction. In transcription, children are asked to imitate what others do and to base learning on what is given to them to learn in a passive, linear way. Transaction, in contrast, asks the child to learn language by using it in transactional and social ways. Experimentation and creativity are promoted as the child flourishes in a world of words. Gradually, as they exchange words with others in their community—and listen to the way language is used—they grow from the transactions and become increasingly competent language users. The alternative to this scenario is transmission, where active transactions with others are replaced with one-way teaching from an omniscient teacher. In this context, learning is controlled, limited, and stymied. Children learn only what is permitted, and the empowerment that accompanies language growth is eliminated. Gradually, our natural love for language—something that emerges from our first years as language users—is replaced with fear, as we stop wanting to make language for others.

In the end, Weaver suggests that the transmission model is at fault because "it does not reflect how children actually learn complex processes" (54). As we know, children learn language by hearing it and using it in their own way and in their own time. When we try to wrest power away from them and tell them how to learn it—and when we impose arbitrary rules about language on them—we make language foreign and unpleasant and stunt a naturally growing process. Language, it seems clear, is not taught but learned as the learners participate in increasingly complicated transactions with language and the people or books that sponsor them.

Design Mind vs. Sign Mind

In her book *Writing the Natural Way*, Gabrielle Lusser Rico discusses the function of the brain's two hemispheres when it comes to using language and the importance of tapping into the right hemisphere. According to Rico, the left hemisphere of the brain is where language is stored but it is the right hemisphere that allows us to express joy and pain and gives us an avenue for emotion. Rico discusses brain research showing that people who lose the function of their right hemispheres—because of strokes or accidents—often lose the ability to laugh or cry and are unable to communicate feelings of grief. She urges us to use our brain's right hemispheres in constructing language, since it is the right hemisphere that produces the poetic and expressive words that are so integral to our early language growth.

It is the right hemisphere that takes risks and exults beauty. It is the right hemisphere that allows us to laugh and cry and use language for personal expression. The expressive aspects of the brain are those that must be activated if we are to continue to grow as language users. "All this suggests," write Lusser Rico, "that the right brain, specialized for patterns, emotions, and open-endedness, has much to do with our aesthetic rendering of the world" (81). Later, she adds the caveat, "as long as we do not call on the specialized talents of both brains to cooperate in writing, we will have to struggle to write naturally" (81).

What Language Acquisition Can Teach Us

We can glean much from the transactional, social, and process-oriented way that children learn language, especially as we consider the way we learn to read and write later in life. It seems clear from all of the research done on language acquisition that we learn to express ourselves by being allowed to learn language in meaningful ways. As children, we acquire language by actively creating models and using them in real-life situations. Along the way, we are given encouragement and plenty of nurturing. Under these circumstances nobody ever fails to learn to speak.

But what happens when it comes to reading and writing? Why is there a literacy crisis when it comes to later language skills? Part of the problem is that schools replace parents, and learning becomes supplanted with teaching. In essence, children are no longer allowed to feel ownership over their learning and often become alienated by the process. I conclude this section with some ideas for how we can read and write more effectively based on the knowledge we have about the acquisition of speech. It is curious that literacy critics, who are eager to discuss plummeting test scores, never seem interested in replicating the incredibly successful setting that children experience as they learn to speak. And yet, it is this environment that results in the most effective language growth and cultivation.

What Readers And Writers Can Learn From Speech

Writing and reading, like speech, should be taught with the learner's values, interests, and culture in mind. No parent would force their child to learn the language of their future teachers—or tell their kids that their language is inferior—but too often schools teach kids to hate their language. This does not mean that formal ways of writing should be ignored. Rather, it means that writers should be taught to write in different contexts and appreciate the diversity of language in various situations. This point brings us back to the issue of culture and language and the importance of inviting kids—and adults—to use their own dialect when processing language. When we encourage linguistic diversity in our writing, we show writers that writing is inclusive and democratic—that it has room for their family's way of speaking.

Again, the metaphor of Frank Smith's "literacy club" is informative in understanding how literacy is learned. Essential for the acquisition of both reading and writing is a context in which children are accepted as legitimate members. Have you ever walked into a place and immediately felt that you didn't belong, that people resented you simply because of the way you were dressed or the words on your sweatshirt? Have you ever been a victim of racism, where people communicated their resentment toward you with looks and barbs and body language? When children enter school and find their dialects or vocabularies are not valued by teachers, they quickly begin to feel that they do not belong in the "literacy club" and that reading and writing is not for them. Through implicit rejection and humiliation, they learn that literacy is not worth the embarrassment or alienation and reject the entire enterprise. They begin to fear the teacher's corrections and resent the red of the pen as it marks every deficiency in the way they learned language. By allowing students to practice writing—and all language skills—with different audiences, we help them to see that their language is sometimes appropriate and that language is a social, living endeavor.

In discussing the transition from home to school, linguist Nigel Hall poses a question that should be asked by any person who is interested in literacy. "What happens when children go to school? Are they able to construct their ideas about literacy in a meaningful manner? Are they going to have a wide range of purposeful literacy?" (73-74).

Unfortunately, continues Hall, the answer is often no. "A range of evidence seems to point to schools providing an environment which conflicts with many young children's beliefs about, and expectations for, print and its use. It appears," laments Hall, "that schools far from continuing to open options about literacy, frequently operate effectively to close such options down" (74). Writer and educator Donald Graves adds to this lament by suggesting, "We ignore the child's urge to show what he knows. We underestimate the urge because of a lack of understanding of the writing process and what children do in order to control it. Instead, we take the control away from children and place unnecessary road blocks in the way of their intentions" (3).

This impediment is non-existent in acquiring speech because children are rarely made to feel like pariahs in their own homes and among their families. But when children begin to learn reading and writing, it is in a context that includes an academic setting and that is rife with concerns that have nothing to do with learning language and that often poisons the linguistic well from which children learn. No longer are kids asked to learn language for their personal goals, but now must take tests and perform for a school that measures their scores against kids from other countries. Instead of being allowed to read and write and enjoy the poetic and personal qualities that it engenders, kids are compelled to take writing and comprehension tests and are timed in doing acts that used to be personally edifying. In such an exploitive and unsettling atmosphere, kids decide to avoid the pain and abandon language.

A good example of how a child's natural language growth, which flourished at home, is blunted and often destroyed is in the government's approach to learning in general. In 1985, the Reagan administration came out with a report on education, which it titled "A Nation at Risk." The major contention of the political document was that our children were not as competitive as they once were and that the effective practices that cultivated learning in past decades were no longer being utilized. What was most unsettling about the document was its obvious perception of kids as nothing more than parts in an international struggle to be powerful and dominate. When the document declared that our nation was at risk because "our once unchallenged preeminence in commerce, industry, science, and technological innovation is being overtaken by competitors throughout the world" (Long 10), we quickly became aware that the authors of the report were concerned with international competition rather than the personal growth and happiness of the school children about whom the document reported.

Learning, we must never forget, is about personal concerns. We do not learn to speak so that one day we can surpass the verbal skills of people in nations that are competing with America, and we do not learn to read and write so we can one day evince our superiority to other people. If we were taught language with such pressure, we would quickly detest the endeavor and try other activities that were closer to our own values. Where speech is learned in a setting that makes the enterprise enjoyable, other skills seem intertwined in international politics and intrigue. Perhaps Mark Twain said it best when he suggested that "if we taught our children to speak the way we teach them to write, everyone would stutter" (Klausser 10).

What About The Real World?

There will always be people who argue that language must be taught in this competitive, impersonal way, since such tactics mirror the way our competitive free-market system works. Such arguments disregard the way people learn and ignore the fact that learning happens more fluidly when it is germane to the person doing it. As a teacher for many years, I learned rather quickly that I could force children to learn facts and skills that were irrelevant and boring to them—because the school forced me to teach them—but the kids would forget it all as fast as they were able to dump it onto the pages of their test. The entire process was meaningless to them and resulted in less learning and even less desire to learn in the future. In the end, too much of this coerced, real-world-force-feeding, only leads to alienation, drop-outs, and less competitive adults for our masterminds in government. We should be wise enough to recognize the effortless way that kids learn speech and emulate that process in teaching reading, writing, and other scholastic endeavors. We should treat language as a natural human activity and stop reducing it to national statistics and international comparisons. Yes, literacy is important and a concern, but to make it into a tense struggle that guarantees losers, increases the chances that our children will never learn language in a productive and personally fulfilling way.

Language Should Be Tied To Experience

We learn to speak because it is a natural reaction to our social lives. In essence, it grows from our experiences. This is the same impetus for learning to read and write and should be central to each endeavor. When kids write in a natural context—one that mirrors their acquisition of speech—they write about aspects of their lives that are relevant, that touch them and matter to them. Much of the same is true for reading. Kids learn to read by exploring ideas and messages that are germane to their existences. When kids are compelled to read and write about topics that are distant from their lives, they become passive and see the act as a departure from the way they learned speech. Quickly, they lose interest in the entire enterprise.

Writing And Reading Should Be Social

This begins with student participation and the acknowledgement that language learning is an ongoing transaction between a person and a text. When children open a book, they merge their system of values—their paradigm of the world—with the words and ideas that lie on the printed page. In reading those words, they bring them to life, creating a personal reading that can never be duplicated because those thoughts and beliefs they have as they read are forever in flux. If you think back to the chapter on reading and literary interpretation, you know that we all read books in different ways, approaching them from personal perspectives. This transaction is also evident when we speak and later when we begin to write. In each instance, the children are applying their own vision of the world to the linguistic experience.

To strip language of this social activity—to denude it of the social interaction between a reader and writer—is to expunge any social aspect from its essence. This happens when we see kids being forced to read books because some day they will appreciate them or to write essays because they need to learn how academics write. This, of course, is standard fare for most language arts classes that have long been inundated with complaints from government officials and worried government imperialists.

Something To Think About

Visit your local school or talk to school administrators and ask them how they approach literacy in their curriculum. Is it based on a series of objectives that reflect the natural way kids learn speech or is it predicated on the objectives of outside forces, such as arbitrary standards established by some government bureaucrat? After the interview, visit the school or obtain a copy of the course description. Does the school respect or even acknowledge the interests of the learner in designing classes and assignments? And, finally, how much emphasis is placed on testing? Of all of the destructive aspects of schooling, none is more harmful than testing. Instead of being assessed by what they do in a stress-free environment, kids are forced to sit in rows and learn facts and perform acts that the school deems important. And, if the child fails to measure up to the expectations of the school, they are punished and branded. They are told they are "learning disabled" or challenged. Of course, when learning to speak in the safe confines of their parents' home, these same kids were given unlimited time to talk and make mistakes, and their success rate was 100%.

Works Cited

Chomsky, Noam. "Interview with Brian McGee." *Men of Ideas*. Ed. Brian McGee. London: BBC Publications, 1979.

Golinkoff, Roberta Michnick, and Kathy Hirsh-Pasek. *How Babies Talk. The Magic And Mystery of Language in the First Three Years of Life*. New York: Plume, 2000.

Graves, Donald. *Writing: Teachers and Children at Work*. Portsmouth, NH: Heinemann, 1983.

Hall, Nigel. *The Emergence of Literacy*. Portsmouth, NH: Heinemann, 1987.

Heny, Jeannine. "Learning and Using a Second Language." *Language Readings in Language and Culture*. Sixth Edition. Eds. Virginia P. Clark, Paul A. Eschholz, and Alfred F. Rosa. New York: Bedford/ St. Martin's Press, 1998. 160-189.

Klauser, Henriette Anne. *Writing on Both Sides of the Brain*. San Francisco: Harper Collins. 1987.

Lenneberg, Eric. *The Biological Foundations of Language*. New York: Wiley, 1967.

Luser Rico, Gabrielle. *Writing the Natural Way*. Los Angeles: J.P. Tarcher, 1983.

Long, Robert Emmet. *American Education*. New York: The H.W. Wilson Company, 1984.

Moskowitz, Arlene. "The Acquisition of Language." *Language Readings in Language And Culture*, Sixth Edition. Eds. Virginia P. Clark, Paul A. Eschholz, and Alfred E. Rosa. New York: Bedford/St. Martin's Press, 1998. 529-555.

Skinner, B.F. *Verbal Behavior*. New York: Appleton-Century-Crofts, 1957.

Smith, Frank. *Joining the Literacy Club*. Portsmouth, NH: Heinemann, 1988.

Weaver, Constance. *Understanding Whole Language*. Portsmouth, NH: Heinemann, 1990.

CHAPTER VI

LANGUAGE: A PERSONAL REFLECTION

Bernadette Gongora, the author of this final chapter, grew up in New York to Cuban-American parents. As a college student, she moved to France and lived and studied there for a year before completing her degree at the University of Miami, in Coral Gables, Florida. Her language experiences in Europe, South America, and in Florida are revealing in what they show us about the politics and learning of language.

...

When I stepped off the airplane in 1973, Miami seemed to my nine-year-old eyes like a sensuous and exotic paradise. Little did I know I'd be thrown into a cultural quagmire which would catapult me into my own personal identity crisis. I had been raised in an eclectic neighborhood in the Bronx, New York, where the mellifluous sounds of each neighbor's language danced in my ears. Each one of my classmates spoke a different language at home and with their relatives, and that was the norm. Neither I, nor any of my friends, were bothered when one would be excluded from the conversation. It was tantamount to being told to go to another room while family discussed issues.

So, when I excitedly arrived at my new school in my Miami, I was horrified to hear the teacher say, "If any students speak Spanish on the playground they will serve detention after school." She then intimated that she would have monitors at undisclosed locations to guard against language violations. I quickly concluded that she didn't like Hispanics for the Spanish they spoke. That's when I asked a classmate what was happening. She turned around and just said the word "PREJUDICE." That was the first time I had heard that word. How could such a lovely sounding word represent such a hateful idea?

That experience haunts me yet today. As I have gained a better understanding of people and their fears, those memories help crystallize the impact it had on me. Today, I understand that language change—like any difference—scares people. It is unsettling to know that difference could replace what is common—that chaos could supplant order. But when it comes to language, the fear is especially acute because language is central to all that we are and have been. It touches our present and has tentacles to our past. My language is who I am and is a mirror into what my family was. It is central to democracy, because through it we are either granted or denied the precious gift of freedom.

So I invite you to journey with me through four continents, hundreds of people, dozens of nationalities and ethnicities—all of which have touched me profoundly. Each continent, each memory, is filled with colorful people and equally colorful languages. I have moments in my life that can only be captured in one language. I have people who will forever be etched in my mind because of the words they whispered to me in their native tongue. To know another language is to know a culture and its people. To be invited into one's language is tantamount to being given an invitation into one's friendship, and I have kinships all over the world.

One Hundred Percent Cuban

As I continued through school in Miami, I quickly realized that I had to identify myself as either Cuban or American. It all began as a rather innocuous incident when I asked a girlfriend where she purchased a tee-shirt that said, **100% Cuban and Proud.**

"I'd like to buy one of those," I said, but she curtly informed me that to don a shirt like hers I would have had to have been born in Cuba.

"I speak Spanish and was born of Cuban parents," I insisted, becoming increasingly perplexed. Needless to say, I never purchased a shirt like many of my classmates and began to wonder who I was and what language I would speak. On one hand, there were the language police who towered around us and admonished us for not speaking English. On the other, there were the children of Cuban immigrants, who accepted only those who were born on the island and who treated others as outsiders. In neither case, it seemed that my language was good or "pure" enough. And yet, it was only through language that I could figure out who I was. To be 100% Cuban meant one was proud of her language, her nation, and her roots. To be American was to speak English and to pronounce words as other Anglos in my class did. I had a decision to make about my identity and much of that decision was wrapped up in the language I chose to speak.

Gradually, I cauterized all ties to the Cuban community, whether it was refusing to speak Spanish or wear the trends that the Hispanics wore. I was what my cousin called, "Una Cubana Arrepentida," and I took great pride in this new label. I knew who I was and that title gave me the right to stand up for my American values, to rebuff all that was tinged with the "inferior" part of my heritage. Later, in high school, I noticed how cliques formed according to how one would dress. The Americans would wear jeans and sneakers, clogs, or boots, while Hispanics donned more formal attire and were in full make up. That wasn't me. Not any longer. Finally, I was feeling comfortable in my own skin. I was American and would speak English in social circles.

I continued to feel more kinship with non-Hispanics and eventually got a job after school. Not very many Hispanics worked, and I found myself alongside predominantly Anglo classmates—first at Burger King and later at a grocery store called Winn Dixie. I loved working. I was more independent than most Hispanic girls my age, and I reveled in the liberty my hard work was earning me.

The Work Place Dilemma—The Right Not To Speak Spanish

Ever since I started working, a feeling of contempt would come over me when I was approached by a Hispanic customer who automatically assumed I would speak Spanish. I would say to myself, "I could be Italian or Greek, why Spanish?" I resented that, and the only way I could rebel is by responding in English. If they wanted to speak to someone in Spanish I would direct them to another colleague or, perhaps, I'd answer them rather coldly. Little by little, I realized that these were customers I'd see on a weekly basis and with whom I'd build relationships. They would come through my line at the same time, a familiar face, a person with whom to chat. They weren't just patrons but acquaintances. And so, one day I decided to stop demanding English from my new friends. I was coming to terms with Spanish and English and refusing to make others feel as alienated as I had once felt.

One Hundred Percent French?

Something about the French language had always intrigued me. It had a melodic sound that moved with the grace of a ballet dancer prancing across a stage. In the seventh grade, I had the option to take French or Spanish; from my history one can gather which one I took. I loved the language and more importantly loved the teacher. Since back in the fourth grade when I had recently arrived from New York and never being exposed to written Spanish, they placed me in the American section, further severing any alliance I would ever foster with the Latin community. During my freshman and sophomore year in high school, I eagerly took French, ready to immerse myself in the language, in every nuance of the culture, its words, and phrases. How disappointed I was when I discovered that the teacher preferred teaching German and showed little enthusiasm for the language for which I felt such passion. I was beginning to see how empty language is when it is devoid of the human aspect. I didn't take French again until I reached the community college and enrolled in a class with a French-born instructor. The next semester she and Dr. Vitale, the abroad program director, became my unofficial mentors, encouraging me to participate in the French program and pursue it with the ardor I had always felt. And so, after finding the linguistic fire still burning, I withdrew all my money, sold my car, and paid my trip and tuition to Aix-en-Provence, France.

Welcome Home

The director kindly assigned me a flat in town where his niece used to live when she was participating in the program. It took longer to load the cab than to drive to my flat. The driver turned around and said, "Voila!" I was baffled, as he had stopped in front of a café. I didn't want to leave for fear he had made a mistake. He grabbed my bags, rather brusquely, I might add, and coaxed me out of the car. When I rang the doorbell, a young lady came down to meet us. She looked at my over-stuffed suitcases and her large brown eyes widened and, then, a faint gasp ensued. She held her three fingers and pointed up. Was I to believe that I was going up three flights of stairs? No, in fact, I was going to go up four because in France they don't count the first floor. Two plump matronly ladies peered over the banister and exclaimed, "Mon dieu!" Just then, my roommate arrived with three suitcases! I don't know how we managed to lug five bags up four flights of stairs, but we did.

The sassy spinsters were lively and vivacious and were both very welcoming. Allyson and I thought we had died and gone to heaven. We were living on the Cours Mirabeau on top of Deux Garcons café-- in the center of town. Our balcony looked over the trees onto the Cours and in the distance I would greet my beloved Mt. Saint Victoire.

A Little Wine Goes A Long Way

Three weeks into my mystically surreal experience, I was invited to a party that was being hosted by some local Tunisians and Algerians. My host mothers warned us about "les pieds noirs." We've never heard of that term before, and we didn't ask until after the party. It was a good thing we didn't because their prejudice might have interfered with a truly wonderful experience. The sisters didn't approve of our attending the party because in France, Algerians aren't seen as French citizens, not truly pure French. They may have been born in France, lived there for decades, and speak the language as their own, but are still unable to be perceived and respected like the French. The term "pieds noirs" sets them apart for merely being born on the African continent, hence relegating them to second-class citizenship. But, we went anyway. We were nineteen and twenty years-old and gloriously naïve, confident nothing would happen because we went in a large, frenetic group.

Just as we assumed, we had an enormous dinner, dessert, and wine—lots of wine. We were cautious because we really weren't familiar with the customs of social occasions. Being from Miami, I was not as trusting as the students from the Midwest and was well-prepared for any monkey business. To my surprise, there wasn't any.

Although I did have a couple glasses, it enhanced rather than impaired my linguistic abilities. I was surrounded by warm, fun-loving people wanting to genuinely know about my life in Miami and what I was doing in France. Gradually, the diminutive and rather timid French speaker inside of me emerged. I was speaking French and feeling like a genuine part of the conversation. Perhaps, it was the collective feeling among us of being outsiders, of knowing that our French—no matter how artful and eloquent—would never meet the standards of our 100% French hosts. Perhaps, it was the sense of mutual acceptance that our French was good enough because it was part of who we were. Whatever it was, the language flowed like French wine, and we left feeling an inner strength and assurance from the night's activities.

The following Monday, I cringed a little less as the teacher methodically hovered around my desk and began to interrogate me in French. Miraculously, as if speaking in tongues, I responded with a fluid torrent of lucid speech. Where I had earlier scrutinized every syllable for its appropriateness, I now felt a surge of confidence that seemed to be rooted in my earlier conversations. My classmates, along with the instructor, were pleasantly bewildered at my new loquaciousness. I was beginning to realize that I had turned the corner that every language user so desperately seeks. I had found my place in the language—a comfortable place where I could speak without fear of rejection. As I slowly realized, speaking French—or any language—didn't guarantee acceptance into the linguistic community. Language was only one part of the cultural dress that one wore each day. It was a ticket into a club, an element of the alchemy, but only a particle. One had to be the right color,and fit the notions of what it meant to be French or Italian or even 100% Cuban. It was, I recognized, very much like my own consternation in Miami. And like that experience, I had to know myself before I could speak the language that was part of my persona.

The Haves And The Have Nots

In 1987, my curiosity veered in a new direction, and I found myself on the mystical shores of South America. I kept telling myself it was a way to polish my waning Spanish, but deep down inside I knew that I was yearning for more of the linguistic buffet I had feasted on in Europe. Again, not knowing a soul except for my advisor, I packed my bags, and headed into a new world, knowing that I would meet new people and languages in this enigmatic and forever perilous land. The enormous difference was quite stark and the urban legends surrounding Colombia were not that incredulous, yet I welcomed each new experience. Being from the U.S., I initially felt some resentment toward me. I assume that my classmates and coworkers were expecting some tall, blue-eyed blond that was going to impose the American culture and humiliate them for having backward ways. They were in no way prepared for me. My unassuming five feet two inches frame along with my dark skin and black curly locks sent them for a loop. I remember traveling to a coworker's hometown for a visit with family. The sister's knowledge of my arrival sent her into fury, and she was going to reserve a room in a hotel until she met me. It was almost suppertime, so we headed for his sister's home. Needless to say, I was warmly welcomed into their home, and the younger daughter readily gave up her bed. We spent that night singing, playing guitar, and drinking agua ardiente. The fiesta went on into the wee hours of the morning. At breakfast, the sister secretly confessed that she was envisioning an imperialist, petulant, overbearing "gringa" that would hardly speak any Spanish. I was really flattered and touched when they went out of their way to make me feel welcomed. That exact scenario occurred time after time. Was I tempting some preconceived notion of what an American looked like? Little by little I started dressing like my classmates and coworkers, and, slowly as time went by, I started picking up the lovely mellifluous accent. Of course, there were some minor changes in vocabulary, but the most notable change was pronouncing every letter in a word. In Carribbean and coastal South American countries, the letter "s" is sometimes omitted. For example, informal Cuban Spanish one would say, "Ven pa ca" but the correct way is, "Venga para aca." As my cultural and linguistic awareness heightened I became more accepting of my Hispanic side.

But, there is one language I thought I knew...the language of poverty. In all my voyages I've never had to confront abject poverty. Walking through the dirty streets of Bogota, emaciated cows staked on barren plots of land, and roaming "gamines" preying on their next victim, either by picking their pockets or mugging them. Children should be enjoying their childhood and not climbing on mounds of debris and wading through filthy puddles at the dump for meager shards of glass. My heart broke when I saw them with bandaged hands and vacuous eyes. I asked my colleague what they were doing in such a precarious environment, and she callously replied, "That's how the poor make ends meet." I was astonished. She went on to say that Colombia along with many South American countries is where the chasm between the affluent and the indigent was more prevalent.

The contact person in Colombia organized several trips during our stay, which helped me glean a better understanding of the word poverty and all of the ramifications that embodies. It wasn't living as a child in a cramped one bedroom apartment with their grandmother, mother, three children and a dog, like I had spent some of my childhood. Despite my mother not being able to use her teaching degree in the U.S. and not being completely proficient in the language, she instilled the importance of receiving a good education, hard work and tenacity. My mom worked several jobs including cleaning toilets, serving lunches and driving a school bus for the local child care center. She took that job because that would allow her to bring us to and from school and have a place to go while she worked.

That wasn't poverty.

Not having all the nice clothes that my classmates had. That wasn't poverty. My mother single-handedly infused determination, resourcefulness, and strength in her three children. The fact is that my siblings and I have had an opportunity to achieve what my mother always dreamed for us. **That's not poverty**.

Poverty is not having the possibility to dream.

When the director took us to a town near the Magdalena River, I witnessed real poverty. This word is diverse in meaning because of the relativity factor. The intrinsic meaning conjures up myriad images of the actual definition. The meaning depends on the person, the upbringing, and experiences. For example, Donald Trump has a different interpretation from a villager in Brazil. So when we traveled to the tiny town roughly several hours from Bogota, we were hospitably welcomed to their homes. There were so many people. We gathered in a courtyard. It was a warm, pleasant evening. We could hear the din of the powerful river raging in the background reminding the inhabitants of her constant threat. We treated them to pop and ice cream in hopes that these lovely people would share their stories of the flood that ravaged their simple houses. As each family recounted their story, everyone's eyes would well up with tears. The community primarily depended on cultivating the land. They were all humble farmers who were just thankful that the mighty river had left their homes unscathed. Many of the people had amassed modern comforts like washers, dryers, televisions, stereos and a few of them had cars. But, as we said our good-byes for the night, Marta and Gilberto, a lovely couple with two little girls shyly said, "Don't feel badly for us because we didn't lose anything of value," referring to people in their community. As I evaluated the evening, I realized that our hosts initially were using the formal usage of "you"/usted but by the end of the soiree they were using the informal/tu. I suppose they felt closer to us because they had shared a personal story.

Ending Comments

Walls. . . They seem to always exist, whether they are erected for political or linguistic reasons. Cubans demanded I be 100% Cuban and later the French warned me about the Algerians and their alien language and customs. Today, we construct similar barriers to the darker people who work in our fields and speak a foreign tongue. What have I learned from my travels, as I sit comfortably on my American sofa and reflect? Perhaps, the most memorable lesson involves my linguistic experiences—from Miami to Paris to Bogota-- and the way they were used—

and abused—to practice the prejudice we still see in our twenty-first century world. A very smart philosopher once said that language, like education, is always political. He was right.

Bernadette Gongora, 2006